THE BOOK OF

BENJAMIN

To Raven,
God Bless you for
the love & support. May
God continue to use
your heart and service
to heal the nation.
Bigmouthben
Benjan C. Goeben
4/6/2018

Bigmouthben

ISBN 978-1-64079-828-1 (Paperback)
ISBN 978-1-64079-829-8 (Digital)

Christian Faith Publishing, Inc.
296 Chestnut Street
Meadville, PA 16335
www.christianfaithpublishing.com

Printed in the United States of America

Dedication

This book is dedicated to my lovely wife, Tanya Graham.

Contents

Acknowledgments 7

1   Introduction..11

2   Seeds of Childhood 13

3   Arriving in Atlanta 17

4   Self-Help Book Discovery 21

5   Discovery of the Street Life 25

6   College Life..29

7   Back to Atlanta..41

8   A Deal with the Devil...44

9   The Birth of Addiction...50

10 Life-Threatening Injury..63

11 Another Relapse 68

12 Birth of the Wheelchair Big Mouth Ben..................77

13 Homelessness 81

14 A Conversation with God 93

15 Metro Day Reporting Center 96

16 Unexpected 104

17 Back into the Music 113

18 My College Sweetheart..116

19 Opening the Store 119

20 The Wedding 124

21 Finale 135

Acknowledgments

First, I must give thanks to God and his precious gift of Jesus Christ and the Holy Spirit.

A very special thank you to the City of Atlanta and its partnering agencies that provided resources for me during my time of need.

Hope Atlanta
Atlanta Union Mission
Mercy Care
The Gateway Center
Making a Way Housing Inc.
Partners for Home

Another special thank you to Larry for his editing services with my manuscript. Thank you to Christian Faith Publishing Inc. for helping me to bring this dream to reality.

A special thank you to all of my family and friends. Your acts of love during my journey proved to be seeds of life to my spirit. I love you all.

To my lovely wife, Tanya Graham, this book wouldn't be without you. From the time we reunited, my life has been complete. I love you, sweetheart.

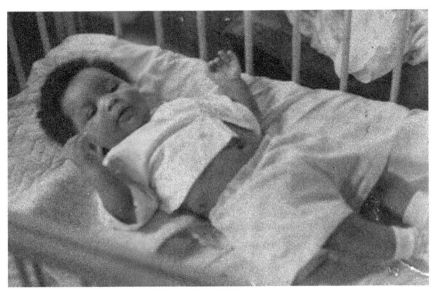

Jeremiah 1:5 (ESV)
"Before I formed you in the womb I knew you,
and before you were born I consecrated you;
I appointed you a prophet to the nations."

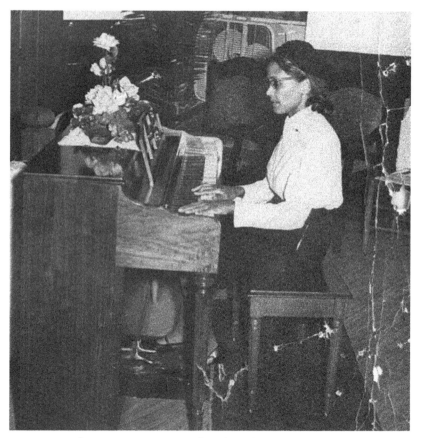

Dora Graham, Benjamin's grandmother playing the piano at Church.

CHAPTER 1

Introduction

Life has a funny way of unfolding. I would never think I would have gone through what I have been through. Now that I look back at all this, I see a beautiful picture coming together. I can surely say that I'm grateful now that it has unfolded before me the way it has.

The purpose of sharing the wonderful details of my life is to inspire you to a purposeful, peaceful, and productive life. The Creator blesses us with this beautiful thing called life. We live, making choices each day, and the sum of those choices pretty much determines our quality of life. It seems so easy! All I have to do is make good choices for a good life. Well, while that's the biggest part; we have to throw in all the other stuff like good and evil, temptation, and any other thing that may railroad us on the way to the good life.

Train up a child in the way he should go, And when
he is old he will not depart from it. (Proverbs 22:6, NKJV)

One thing I can conclude while summarizing my life up to this point is that it has truly been a spiritual journey. I learned early about God and the way I should go. I can't say that I stayed on that path, but I never gave up believing that God would somehow continue to love me in spite of it all.

The *Book of Benjamin* is similar to other books in the Bible, such as the book of Job and others. This is a book about my walk with the Lord throughout my life. Here are the accounts of my life from birth to present. I must warn you that my walk wasn't a perfect one. This story shows a stray from the path, but another chance to get it right. I urge you to personalize this story to your own life. You don't have to travel in my shoes to experience the joy that is available to those that realize where their heart should be. I love you all. Enjoy the *Book of Benjamin*!

CHAPTER 2

Seeds of Childhood

W ho doesn't remember their childhood? Our childhoods are the very essence of who we are today. In my case, seeds were planted that shaped who I have become. I want to start with the good stuff. My spiritual foundation was laid from the start. I was raised by a God-fearing grandmother. Grandma was a schoolteacher and the church pianist. Many hours were spent worshiping God. I received Christ at an early age, and I believe that everyone should love each other like Christ loves us. Music went right along with the spiritual seeds. Right now, I have a pleasant memory of dancing at the age of three to the first song I remember as "Tie a Yellow Ribbon 'Round the Oak Tree." My passion for music was obvious as I played the drums in church at the age of six. Music was one of the talents God gave us. As Grandmother played and I beat the drums, people shouted, filled with the Holy Spirit.

The seed of entrepreneurship was planted in me at the age of six as well. While in the gas station, I observed a gentleman return an empty Coke bottle and the cashier gave him some money. My eyes grew big at this and I asked why was he giving him money for an empty bottle? His response was whenever someone brought in these Coke bottles, they would receive money. I told him I knew where to find those bottles. I ran home, grabbed my red wagon, and went to work. While the other kids played, I looked for empty bottles. I collected unwanted bottles from the neighbor's yard and off the streets and took my first load of bottles to the gas station. I was paid two dollars for my first load, and I was excited. I bought two dollars' worth of bubble gum, ran into the woods, and laughed. Making money was that easy. I actually did something that grown people do. I made money. I was hooked on making money from that day!

The positive seeds in my life, spiritual, music, and business were planted as early as age six. As you know, evil is somewhere lurking in the background, tempting people to commit horrible acts. I was a victim of this evil. While on my search for empty bottles, I wondered onto the property of someone evil. He said I was trespassing and shouldn't be in his yard. I was raised to have good manners, so I quickly apologized and attempted to leave, but he said that I had to be punished. He grabbed me and told me in order to leave, I had to do something for him. This scared me. He grabbed me by my hands and took me further in the woods. I tried to escape, but he held on tight to my arms. Once we were deeper in the woods, he removed his pants and told me if I didn't do what he wanted, he would kill me. At the age of six, I was molested and forced to have oral sex. Afterward, I ran out the woods and into my house. My grandmother knew something had happened. She begged me to tell her what happened. I feared for my life and hers, so I made up a lie. I told her I was in the woods, and a lizard crawled up my leg. She believed me. I could not stop shaking from this ordeal. I felt dirty! I went into my room a wept quietly.

"Lord, why did this happen to me!" I prayed. "I thought you loved me and would protect me wherever I went?"

I was confused. This incident contributed to a whole lot of self-destructive behaviors later on in my life. I kept this horrible secret until it was mandatory to talk about it in order to get sober later on in life.

"Why did people act like this?" I asked the Lord, but I guess I didn't understand His answer at that age, so I just buried the secret in my heart and kept moving.

I was also exposed to my grandfather's abuse of my grandmother. My grandfather was an alcoholic. He would get drunk and beat my grandmother four times a week! I started to feel like Grandmother would get punished for going to church. How could this be? I thought church was supposed to bring good things, but what I saw was that going to church brought pain to my grandmother, and the church didn't protect me from being molested. I started to develop some rebellion against God. I myself started to experiment with cigarettes and alcohol at the age of seven. Granddaddy was too drunk to keep track of what he drank and smoked so I would help myself to left-overs. My smoking habit increased as I was collecting bottles to buy a pack of cigarettes. Back then, there was no law against minors buying cigarettes; besides, they knew my grandfather was always sending me to buy them for him. They would have never suspected that they were for me! I guess I learned self-destructing ways of coping at an early age.

My prayers at that age were "Dear God, why are people so evil? Why do they do bad things to other people. Why is my grandfather beating my grandmother? She loves you. Can't you make it stop? They say You can do everything. Why do You keep letting her go through this?"

If God answered, I don't think I heard him or I was too young to understand. This way of life continued for a couple a years.

I began to act out in school. Grandma began to receive reports on my behavior from other teachers. She would get upset at this. I wasn't a bad student. I would mostly get in trouble for talking too much and not being still. That later became an asset for me as I grew older. I can't remember the exact day and time, but I was called out of class by the principal. He told me something had happened to my grandmother. She had a heart attack and was rushed to the hospital. I sat in the office, waiting on my grandfather to pick me up. When we arrived at the hospital, we were told to wait in this room. A doctor came out to speak with us. He said they tried everything, but couldn't save my grandmother. I didn't believe it. I just knew when we got home, Grandma would be cooking dinner in the kitchen. I jumped out the cab and ran into the house.

"Grandma? Where are you?" I yelled even louder.

I thought Granddaddy and the doctor were playing a joke on me. Granddaddy began to yell for me to calm down. At this point, it started to sink in that Grandma was gone. I went in my room, and I cried. I decided to pray again. "Lord, why did you take Grandma? She was the only good one in this house." This became my first encounter with losing someone close.

The funeral was held a week later. My mother came up from Atlanta with my two younger brothers that I would meet for the first time in person. I hugged her and my brothers and started back crying. "I want my grandma!" is what I repeated over and over. Mother seemed to comfort me during this time. She said I would be going back to Atlanta with her where we all could be together. It all seemed unreal at first, but to see my grandmother lying in a casket unresponsive was the reality of it all. I can remember then trying to fall down the steps. I wanted to go with her. Was this my first attempt of suicide? Not sure, but I knew I wanted to go wherever she was.

CHAPTER 3

Arriving in Atlanta
More Childhood Seeds

Atlanta seemed too big. We came in on the Greyhound bus. I saw these huge buildings and a lot of cars that seemed to be in a hurry. All the rushing and traffic. My introduction to the city was the radio playing KC and the Sunshine Band's "Shake Your Booty." Of course, I hadn't heard too much soul music. I was raised up on gospel music. My memory of this song was Atlanta is jamming! We finally arrived at the bus station in Atlanta where one of Mother's friends picked us up and took us to their home where we spent a few months until Mother could move us into an apartment at East Lake Meadows. I had to adjust to having brothers. I was used to sleeping in a bed by myself, but at my mom's friend's house, all three of us sleep in the same bed. I can remember my first night there, arguing with my brothers about who is going to sleep in the middle. We made Brandon sleep in the middle. He was the youngest, I was the oldest, Romero next, and then Brandon.

When we settled down in East Lake Meadows, I was happy that Momma finally had her own apartment. We all shared a bedroom while Mom had her room. Our uncle also shared this apartment with us, and at the time, it was good for Momma because he would watch us while Momma worked. Uncle had been to Vietnam, and the results, as I now look back, affected him in various ways. His idea of raising boys up to be men would today fit into the category of child abuse. Even today, he tells the story of my arriving in Atlanta with a walk that was too suspect for a boy at that age. He claim that he had to intervene by exposing me to some females. His idea? I was locked in a bedroom with some *Playboy* and *Penthouse* magazines at eight years old and told I couldn't come out of the room until I looked at every page. By the age of ten, I had become obsessed with porn and looking at naked women in magazines. My uncle said that we also had to be tough to live in East Lake Meadows, so he would make sure we fought the other kids in the neighborhood. He said he wasn't raising no wimps! I was forced to bully others and treat the girls rough. My uncle hustled as a pimp, so he wanted to raise some young pimps as well. My spirit didn't agree with treating people like this, but as a ten-year-old, what could I do? I didn't want to get beaten by my uncle, so I had to do what he told me. I think even some of this treatment to a certain degree did help me with dealing in the streets because I was one person that wouldn't scare easy, but for the most part as being exposed to counseling, I conclude that this abuse only made things worse for my overall character. I can remember getting sent home from school for throwing someone in the creek doing recess. Instead of getting punished for bullying, my uncle told me I did a good job and I could sit at home with him and watch TV. My uncle wanted to raise a gangster. Thank you, Lord, for intervening!! We tried to tell Mom at times of the abuse but was too afraid of making her unhappy or getting my uncle in trouble, I guess. When looking back at this, I forgive and understand that my uncle suffered his own mental illness from the war. Unfortunately, no one in our family believed in "crazy medicine" or treatment for mental health. The cycle continued for another two years.

"Dear Lord, why is my uncle so mean? Why does he make us beat other up kids? Forgive us, Lord, and help us to get away from him."

704 Hobart Street

Our move to 704 Hobart Street was like an escape from Uncle. It was a house in the Grant Park area. I think I was about twelve at the time. I still felt we was poor as children, but it wasn't that Mom didn't work. She had a great job as budget analysis at GA Tech. It was the fact she had to pay all the bills and raise us as well. Mom was a strong woman who raised us, and she did a great job. She made sure we did good in school, and if we didn't, we were punished (in a good way of course. Nothing like Uncle). I can never remember starving as a kid. We always had clothes even if they were from the thrift store. Mom made sure we had something different to wear every day. The Grant Park area bought more friends and more positive seeds in the childhood. My love for music blossomed as I took on the endeavor of learning to play the string bass. I was introduced to classical music. I loved this music. There was something calming about it. Creating beautiful music was always calming.

Be ye strong therefore, and let not your hands be weak:
for your work shall be rewarded. (2 Chronicles 15:7)

We couldn't afford instruments, so I chose the string bass because the school had one available. In order to practice at home, I had to carry the bass from the school, which was a three-mile walk. I was so determined to learn the instrument that I didn't care about walking this distance with a thirty-pound string bass. I spent many tiring days toting that heavy bass back and forth. The teacher drove past me one day while I was walking home. She noticed that I would walk a ways and then rest. The next day in school, she called me in her office and explained how she admired my determination and allowed me to keep one string bass at home and practice in school with a second one. One character trait I credit God for giving me, and that was stubborn determination. I was willing to work hard for what I wanted, and it wasn't easy for me to accept it when someone told me I couldn't do it. I had to prove them wrong. Determination!

3025 Pasadena Drive

Here is where the rest of my childhood would reside. After a few years of renting, Momma finally achieved the American Dream. She bought a house. It was located at 3025 Pasadena Drive, and it was huge, at least to us it was. It had a basement and a big backyard. We all were so happy. We had our own rooms and space to play. I continued my schooling and participation in orchestra at Knollwood Elementary School.

Benjamin Graham at 12 years old with his younger brothers and sisters Sami, Brannon, Benjamin, Romero, Tammy, and Henson (front)

CHAPTER 4

Self-Help Book Discovery

My discovery of self-help books came at the age of thirteen. While rambling in my mother's bedroom, I discovered some books under her bed. Being curious, I began to read them. My first book was *The Magic of Believing* by Claude Bristol. My mother never knew that I had the books. I had become obsessed with this mind stuff. I thought of it to be magic. I actually thought that I could develop some magic by projecting my thoughts. I read the chapter on how to project your thoughts and began my mission. I thought to myself that there was a million dollars buried in our backyard. I would concentrate on that thought for three days. I made a list of things I wanted and had my younger brothers do a list too. On the fourth day, we began to dig. We dug and dug until we had a giant hole in our backyard. Mom began to yell at us, wondering what in the world we were doing. I quickly told her that she wouldn't have to work no more because I had projected my thoughts! I told her about finding her book and reading it. She took one look at what I was explaining to her and began to laugh. She then explained to me how self-help books really worked, that it wasn't instant-type magic, but more of having a positive attitude and that was the magic they were talking about. This didn't discourage me from reading. I went on to read other books like *Think and Grow Rich* by Napoleon Hill. My grades in school increased. People labeled me the positive thinker. I was always trying to uplift my friends. Most of them laughed at me, but I didn't care. I knew that a positive attitude would one day take me to the top.

Work Hard

The entrepreneurial spirit never left me. I grew up with a money-making attitude. I can remember coming home crying one day because the local grocery store said that I was too young to work. They told me to come back in two years, and to me, that was too long to wait. Mom told me I would have to get creative. I began to canvas the neighborhood for work such as raking yards and cutting grass. I enjoyed the feeling of having my own money. I knew my mom was still struggling with bills, so I wouldn't ask her for anything. Whatever I wanted, I would save up and buy. I remember once being interested in metal detecting. I saw my friend with one, and I set my mind to save up my money and buy me one. I learn to set goals from the books I was reading. I went door to door seeking work from the neighbors. After a few jobs, I was able to buy my metal detector. Mom was proud.

Music

Another hobby at the age of twelve was music. I love music. Any kind of music suited me, classical, pop, rhythm and blues, you name it, I loved it. I started collecting records. I would do odd jobs in the neighborhood and travel to downtown Atlanta and buy my records. My collection began to grow as so did my interest in being a disc jockey. We had an empty storage room in the basement. We nicknamed it the dark room because it was just that, a dark room full of things left behind from the previous homeowners. One day, we decided to clean it out. Once we had everything out, we decorated the walls and the room became our club. We set tables up for the turntables. Mom was impressed with what we did to the room, so she went out and bought a strobe light. We had our first party in the basement. Our neighborhood friends came out and enjoyed the party. After playing music that day, I knew I wanted to be a DJ. My best friend and I formed a rap group and we began our quest.

High School

I matured fast while in high school. I attended Avondale High School. My first year there, I attempted to try out for the basketball team but was not quite sure of myself. I really wanted to play football, but Mom was fearful of my skinny bones being broken in two. I eventually ended up in the marching band. I actually chose to learn the trombone. Like my journey with the string bass, I had to carry my trombone from the house to school every day, which was a four-mile hike each way. I didn't mind. I really wanted to be good enough to march on the field during the half-time show. I put in months of hard work. Finally, the day approached for my tryout to be in the Marching Blue Devils Band. Nervous but confident, I entered the room and aced my audition. I was a member of the marching band! I shared this news with Mom, and she was so proud and excited.

"I told you that you can do whatever you put your mind to. I love you, baby."

Most of the things I went after with hard work and determination became a reality. I truly believe that you have to put in the work to get what you want out of life.

School was great, but I was starting to feel depressed because I didn't have money to do or have the things I wanted. Band activities had a cost, and I was constantly asking Momma for these things. She simply couldn't afford it. We had a break from marching season, so I began to look for work. I was only fifteen, but I had a work permit. My best friend Spud was working at McDonald's. He put in a few words for me, and I had my first job! Mom was excited but said if my grades dropped, I would not be working there next quarter. The job was several miles from the house. I rode my bike there. I was so excited to have a job that I worked as long as I could. Management was pleased and gave me more hours. I would get out of school at 3:00 p.m. and go to work at McDonald's until closing time, 11:00

p.m. I got home around 1:00 a.m., studied when I had to until 3:00 a.m. I was able to work and remain on the honor roll. Determination.

My love for the marching band started to conflict with my working at McDonald's, and as a result, management scheduled me for one day a week! I wanted more hours, but I loved what music did for me. I was a part of something creative. Eventually because of lack of availability, I lost my job at McDonald's and continued on in the marching band.

Summertime came around, giving me more time off, and I got a job at Baskin Robbins. Once again, back on a job and feeling grown up about it. I caught on pretty fast and quickly rose to manager at the age of seventeen. Having been exposed to goal setting from the books I read, I quickly began to set goals for myself. I achieved the American dream of getting my driver's license. I was ready to drive and explore the world! Mom would let me drive her car to the store, but I wanted so badly to have my own car. I went to a "Buy here pay here lot," but because I had no credit, I had to get a cosigner, who ended up being my uncle Mac. They told me that if I could put down 900 dollars, I could take it home. I told them to give me another week. I went to work long hours at Baskin Robbins to complete my goal. One week later, I had enough money to put down on my first car. I had my own car! Determination.

CHAPTER 5

Discovery of the Street Life

I t wasn't shortly after I got my car that I began to ride and explore the streets of Atlanta. Although I love music and school, I seemed to be driven to the streets. I took a ride downtown with my best friend and our younger brothers. The four of us riding around downtown. We drove down Peachtree and made our way over to Auburn Avenue. I remember Auburn Avenue from the times Mom would take us to the Auburn Festival, but from the driver's seat, Auburn Avenue looked so different. It looked tempting! The street was full of women walking around in their lingerie or underwear. We rode up and down the streets for hours staring at these women. We quickly figured out what was going on. These women were prostitutes, and to me, they looked so pretty. I couldn't quite figure out why they weren't married and living in nice homes. Around 1:00 a.m., we decided to head home, but I couldn't shake the thought of the women walking gracefully up and down Auburn Avenue. Temptation prevailed as I went along with the plan to go home, but after dropping everyone else off, I would sneak back downtown. Thoughts ran through my head about the days Uncle made me look at these type women in the magazines. I went back to Auburn Avenue and built up to courage to speak to one of the ladies. From our previous visit, we learned that whenever we were asked if we wanted to date, that meant did we want to pay for sex. I drove slowly down Auburn, turning left on

Fort Street, building up the courage to actually go through with the whole date thing.

A deep Southern voice shouted into the passenger window, "You wanna date, handsome?"

Without thinking, I said yes. She said it would cost me twenty-five dollars, and she got in the car and told me where to park. She told me her name was Strawberry. We parked in the parking lot of some apartments. Nervous but trying to look like I had done it before, we walked up the steps and into an apartment. The whole apartment had an odor.

Speaking to a gentleman that was sitting in front of the television, Strawberry said, "I got a date, Sweets, here you go."

She handed him $5, which apparently was the fee to use the room for a few minutes. I went into the room, and I guess within a matter a minutes, she figured out that I didn't know what I was doing. She took control and guided me through the process. Seven minutes later, it was true! I was no longer a virgin. I felt dirty and proud at the same time, which would be a pattern to my character for a long time. I arrived home at about 3:00 a.m. and went quickly to the bathroom to clean myself off from this adventurous journey on Auburn Avenue. As I removed my underwear, I discovered that she had a put a condom on me. I didn't even notice at the time because I was so nervous! I removed the condom, cleaned up, and went to bed proud.

The next day came and I drove to school with my brother and friends, acting as if nothing had happened outside of our normal trip down there. This secret only lasted about two hours. I had to tell my best friend about my adventure.

"Hey, Spud. You know when I dropped you all off last night, I went back down there …"

Spud didn't believe me at first, but judging by my demeanor and excitement, he was convinced, and then he got mad for not taking him back with me. So we set out to go on the adventure together again the next night. Looking back on my life, I realized that somewhere in time, I developed an addictive personality. Everything I did, I had to overdo. Our adventures on Auburn Avenue happened four times a week. I can truly say that this was an addiction for me. High school girls no longer attracted me. I was hooked on grown women. This probably had something to do with my uncle forcing porn on me at the age of eight. This addiction would carry on into my first year of college. One would ask, how could I afford to travel to Auburn Avenue four times a week to pay for sex. Between working and hustling candy at school, I made enough money to afford my adventure. I had started selling candy at school on the side, but instead of saving the money, I spent it on the prostitutes of Auburn Avenue.

> *"Who have left the straight paths to walk in dark ways." (Proverbs 2:13)*

My journey with God seemed to be growing apart as I took hold of the streets. It's not that God ever leaves us. I believe we leave him when we are drawn away by other desires.

My hanging in the streets after work became a regular routine. I managed to operate off four hours of sleep. I would get off work around 11:00 p.m., hang in the streets of Atlanta until 3:00 a.m., and get up around 7:00 a.m. for school. By hanging in the streets so much, I began to witness violent acts. I saw a man stabbed by another during a fight. I witnessed robberies, violent beatings of the women that worked the street, and petty crimes such as thieves breaking in the cars after the men would park to go inside with the women. The streets seemed to have this attitude of hate and evil. It didn't care about no one, and everyone seemed to be looking for a quick and easy way to make money even if it meant taking it from someone else. In spite of the hate and violence, the pimps on Auburn seemed to find favor in me. They saw my curiosity and told the surrounding aggressors that I was never to be touch or victimized. I felt special. I vaguely remember the downtown with Uncle, but I think a few of them knew that I was his bloodline. Although there was this gravitation toward the street life, my spirit wouldn't rest easy with the idea of having a life in the streets. I thought long and hard. Looking at the painful faces of the women and struggling drug addicts gave me enough convincing to make plans to go down the right path in life.

By my senior year in high school, plans seemed to be plentiful to the point of confusion. I wanted to do so many things to become successful. At first, I was led to join the Air Force. I took the written exam and was informed that I would have to come down take the physical and sign up for my commitment to enlist for a period of four years. I was excited that I would be doing something productive with my life. That following Friday before the day of the physical, I received an acceptance letter from the University of Georgia. Mom was worried about my signing up for the Air Force so the decision was made. Here I come University of Georgia! My trips to Auburn Avenue were on hold with my car's motor locking up. I couldn't afford the repairs, so the car remained parked in my mom's driveway.

CHAPTER 6

College Life

Mom was so proud to have her oldest child heading off the college. By this time, Mom had gotten married to Sam Willingham. Sam and I had our moments, but for the most part, it was all love. We got a late start with the paperwork as for as applying for the dorms, so Mom went all out to make sure I got a good start in school. She rented a one-bedroom apartment and let me have her second car, a 1978 Dodge Aspen. This was the life! Finally own my own with a car and my own apartment. The freedom would get the best of me. I hung out on the campus and got to know everyone I could. Being from Atlanta seemed to have its good points to the locals and college students. I became popular in school pretty fast, having my own car and apartment. The first year actually turned out to be a party year for me. My first quarter grades were extremely poor. I can recall being awaken with a phone call from my mother fussing about how bad I did in school. After the first quarter, I was placed on academic probation. My mother sounded hurt, and I didn't like that. I immediately began to change my tune when it came to partying without studying. My grades began to get better as I pay more attention to the teachers and did the work. My mom was doing so much for me, paying my rent, car insurance, sending me pocket money, and school fees. I think it was around the third quarter that I knew I had to take responsibility for my life. Having gone a few weeks without talking to my mother, I decided to call her to talk. It was at this moment I knew my mom was once again struggling. I dialed the number and got a message that the phone number had been disconnected due to nonpayment. My heart sank. Mom was not paying her bills to make sure I remained in school and in my apartment! From that moment on, I decided I would take full responsibility for my school and apartment. I went job hunting and got my first job while in college. It wouldn't be long before I would add more jobs to my schedule. Within two months, I ended up with several jobs. My schedule was as follows: 4:00 a.m.-8:00 a.m., I would work at United Parcel Service. From 9:00 a.m. to 1:00 p.m., I would work at Bojangle's Chicken and Biscuits. From 2:00 p.m. to 5:00 p.m., I would go to school. From 6:00 p.m. to 10:00 p.m., I would work at McDonald's. I topped all of that off with a final job at DuPont Textile plant on the weekends. Actually, my grades got better with all this working. I had no time to play. I became so focused with my life that focusing in school became easy.

College Photo of Benjamin Graham also known as "Benji K" at University of Georgia.

Music

Of course, my love for music never left me. I didn't pursue any of the orchestral groups, but I did take a liking to disc jockeying. I was making good money for a college student during this time. I invested in some equipment and was soon known as Benji K, the rapper/disc jockey. My popularity grew fast. Along with my jobs, I worked at the radio station from 10:00 p.m. to 12 midnight on Tuesday and Club O'Maleys on Wednesday night. I produced my own records and would test them out at the radio station and club. I have always worked very hard. I would get off at the radio stations at midnight and put up posters in the dorms till around 2:00 a.m. only to get a couple hours of sleep before going to UPS to work. As far as I can remember, I have been a determined person. I didn't believe in not making it. I learned from the self-help books that success is the result of hard work and positive thinking. Determination is the fuel of success. It adds drive to your efforts. It ignores the possibility of failure and keeps trying until success is present. It was amazing how fast my popularity grew as a DJ and rap artist. All my marketing efforts paid off. Benji K became famous in Athens, Georgia. I was soon having a contest at the radio station of winning a date with Benji K. Everywhere I went, people knew me, and boy, did it feel good. I began to see my name in the local papers, and people were asking me to sign their cassette tapes that they bought at the record shops around town. I created those tapes by buying blanks from the tape warehouse and dubbing them until I had enough to take to the stores on consignment. Even during this time, I was operating my own record label. I started my own publishing company with BMI. Determination.

I performed at the Earth Day events, opened up for Grove Trolls, and eventually it led to opening for the famous De La Soul. This show was a great experience. I had my own dressing room, and another great point about this show is that I got paid. When starting out, I would perform for free to get known. This day was quite different in that there were so many artists in the rap game that they started charging them to perform. Can you believe that? You agree to pay a promoter to perform at a club which benefit the people there. I've done it myself, but I didn't see this happening too many times. The show with De La Soul got me a front page with the *Red and Black* newspaper. I often search their database to attempt to retrieve that article, but can't find it. Internet was not quite on the scene in 1988, so not I am not sure if *Red and Black* kept up with the past issues.

I continued to perform, work, and study at the University of Georgia.

Having been raised by a God-fearing grandmother and a hard-working mom, my attitudes toward drugs was very negative. I didn't like them or people that did them. I was raised by a grandmother who was abused several times a week by my grandfather who was an alcoholic. My experience with alcohol started out small and escalated. I thought it made me the life of the party. I began to get drunk and bold. I found myself dancing wild and getting even more attention. My popularity was growing and wasn't easily accepted by the local guys in the streets of Athens, Georgia. They became jealous of my success and determination and began to interfere. One night at the local club, about six of the guys attempted to jump on me. Knocking me down and hitting me with sticks and pipes. I managed to get the pipe from one of the guys and began to fight back. Afraid of going to jail, they cowardly ran off into the night, but I was changed at that point. I felt violated in a major way and vowed to never be in that position again. I made myself a promise that on my twenty-first birthday, I would buy a gun. The only problem with this is that I had being jumped by six guys on my mind when I bought my first gun which happened to be a tech-22 with a 30-round banana clip. This gun was so fast that it was actually recalled because the trigger action was considered to be that of an automatic. I was able to unload thirty rounds in six seconds. I never wanted to get caught slipping again. I rode around in my Delta 88 Oldsmobile with the gun in the seat. A funny thing about the streets is that you can try hard to mind your own business, but usually someone is going to try you and you will have to prove yourself. This is not a good thing because it leads to murder, incarceration, hospital visits, and other painful stuff. I personally don't think the streets will ever change because of the drugs that are in the streets. Most people are always under the influence, not thinking rational in the first place when conflict occurs.

I managed to develop a reputation for holding my own. I would get drunk and waved my assault gun around a couple times to let them know I mean business, and soon, I became known as that crazy guy from Atlanta. People began to fear me, and for some weird reason, it felt good. So here I am, college student, entertainer, and a wannabe gangster. Alcohol had begun to cloud my judgment. I was still working hard and studying, but also driven by this new street image. My relationship with God was growing even further apart.

My First Arrest

It was a late night Tuesday. My younger brother and his best friend was visiting from Atlanta. They were so impressed with the college and how much I had accomplished. I showed them the radio station, and we all had a good time as I did my two-hour disc jockeying spot. After the show, we were walking through the parking lot when I decided to show off my new toy. I took my gun out the bag and emulated the last scene in the movie *Colors* where the two gang members are on the ground on their knees facing each other. I fired several shots into the night. Orange flames were shooting out of the chamber as I released the rounds. My brother and his friend was impressed; scared, but impressed. It was about two minutes after that, that the police came running down the hill at me. I froze as they yelled and screamed for me to get down on the ground. I did as they asked and was immediately taken into custody.

This was a very scary moment for me. I thought, how foolish could I be? Questions plagued my mind. Would I get thrown out of school? Would I be fired from the radio station? What would Momma say? Will I go to prison for this? As I was taken to the Clarke

County Jail, I used my free phone call and called my aunt Goody. She immediately scolded me for my foolishness and placed bail. I was released within a few hours. The school decided to suspend me for two quarters for committing a crime on campus. My charges? Discharging a weapon in public place, carrying a concealed weapon without a license. I would still participate in activities around the campus without them knowing of course. Besides, I was known as Benji K, the famous rapper and disc jockey.

When looking back at these days, I will say that I had become arrogant with all the fame and fortune. The fortune was no more than the money I earned from working five part-time jobs. They outweighed my expenses, 5 to 1. In other words, I had money to blow. Whenever there were major parties and I was performing at these parties, I rented a limo to pick me up and ride around town for a few hours. This made me look even bigger! People loved Benji K, and I loved that attention.

My first introduction and struggle with drugs came from over-working myself. The restaurant I was working at changed management and was run by a family that were into taking drugs. They smoked weed, popped pills, and did whatever else. One day, they started to notice that I was coming to work sluggish in the mornings. I just finished a 4:00 a.m. to 8:00 a.m. shift of lifting boxes at UPS, and by the time I came to work at 9:00 a.m., I was exhausted. I noticed they always talked about speed, a pill nicknamed white crosses. They suggested that I take two pills. They said it would give me a boost. They told me it was just like a cup of coffee without the liquid. I decided to try to two pills. Within minutes, I was perky and working like a race horse. I love this feeling. I didn't feel sluggish or down. I felt upbeat and full of energy! Several hours went by and I started to feel real tired. I guess I was coming down from the speed rush. The next day, I purchased a bottle of thirty pills and began to take as prescribed, whenever I wanted to.

Weeks passed with this incredible new discovery of speed. It wouldn't be long before I began progressing in my addiction of speed. I went from needing two pills every four hours to needed six pills every two hours. I noticed that I began to get mad when things prevented me from moving quickly. My patience went out the window. I began to smash things because I was mad. I finally realized that the speed was hurting more than helping me. I decided to quit. Once I stop, I became so tired. I went home from working at Bojangles to taking a nap before going to school. I slept for the rest of the day, missing school and my scheduled hours at McDonald's that night. I continued to sleep through my UPS morning shift and Bojangles. By this time, people began to worry. They saw my car parked in the apartment complex, but didn't hear from me those two days. Someone decided to call the police. They obtain the keys from the manager of the complex and entered my apartment. I was awakened by constant shaking from the officer.

"Sir? Are you okay? Can you hear me? Do you know where you are?"

I asked what day was it, and they told me it was Wednesday. I actually slept two days and couldn't hear anyone banging on the door. They thought I was in my apartment dead. I slept just that hard. From that point on, I began to live without the help of speed. I slowly watched the restaurant began to go down in business from all the drugs the management was doing. I thought it best to quit that job and get away from them. No sooner than two months after I left, the restaurant went out of business. I wonder why?

Recovering from my bout with speed wasn't that bad as I remember. I believe alcohol might have lessened the withdrawal pains. I quickly went from one addiction to another. From childhood, I hated the taste of beer and alcohol, but for some reason, in college, I began to force the liquor down in order to get drunk. Getting drunk gave me that feeling of being on top or at least I thought so. I also believe that the alcohol was a way to numb the pain from childhood memories in the woods of North Carolina. It made me feel confident to talk to others. It brought me out my shell. It also made me sick, but being, I thought that it was all part of the fun. My drinking began to increase. I drop my schedule at the University of Georgia to part-time because I was paying my own way through and couldn't afford to go full-time. As I think about it, I probably could have paid my way through, but my drinking was causing me to lose focus.

The more I drank, the more violent I became, and I credit the alcohol with my apparent foolish so-called thug activities. I already had a street reputation of being this crazy guy from Atlanta, so once I drank, I would do my best to live up to this. I can remember getting a phone call from a girl that I worked with at McDonald's, saying that her boyfriend had slapped her at the job. I left my apartment with my tech22 semi-automatic weapon and began to head over to McDonald's. Here it is 5:30 p.m., and I enter the restaurant with my gun drawn and pointed it at her abusive boyfriend. People were screaming and running out the restaurant. The managers were begging for me not to shoot him. He was begging also. I made him apologize to her and leave the store. Management begged me to leave so I left. Why didn't anyone call 911? To this day, I don't know, but I added this foolish stunt to the God's grace and mercy category. In Athens, there was only one other person that was as crazy as me and we ended up bumping heads. While at a skate party, people began to tell me that Dex was talking about me. I began to talk about and threaten him. I told his people what I would do if I saw him in the street. Well, that chance came after the party. Krystals was a popular hangout after parties at the club or skating rink. Everybody was hanging out. I rode through in my kitted-up Oldsmobile, rings on every finger hanging out the window. As I parked, someone ran up to me and told me Dex was there and planning on shooting me. Rather than respond in a fearful manner, I began to get upset and angry. I went back to my car and got my gun. People knew what was about to happen, so they began to leave or take cover. All I knew was I saw him walk out the restaurant, and I fired four shots directly at him. People starting screaming and running. Cars were speeding to get out of the parking lot. Dex never returned fire. Luckily, no one got shot. I got back in my car and sped off. People talked about this incident for days. So what type of person was I really? I am still in school majoring in journalism. My dreams were to go into broadcasting, maybe become this famous DJ. I was still working five jobs. Was I really a bad person? No! I was just acting stupid off the alcohol. The alcohol was a demon that possessed me and told me I was unstoppable, that everyone should bow to me. It is quite awesome today to look back over this and realize the spiritual realm of it all. I guess this is why I did not fear anyone in the streets. I know that 99 percent of it is a mask that we wear or either the influence of a drug or alcohol, and because of that, today I am committed to intervening by attempting to connect with the real part of that person. The only problem with today is that there are way more guns and drugs and people are under more than just alcohol.

One day, while I was working at KFC, Dex came into the restaurant and apologized for the beef that we had. He said that he was known for running Athens and felt that I was trying to take his title. I began to apologize as well. His real reason for coming by the store was to recruit me. He told me he had a connect that would front him keys of cocaine, and he needed someone fearless like me to help him build an empire in Athens. I knew nothing about the drug business. Nor did I want to. My opinion back then was that it was a weak thing to indulge in or sell. This was around 1988. I told him that we were cool and no more beef would arise between us, but I was going to continue to pursue my education and work for a living. He accepted my answer and went on to attempt to build his drug dealing business. About three months later, I heard a story about him being robbed and shot in the head for those keys of cocaine. Dex was dead. The news was sad, but I had a feeling of joy that I did not team up with this person. I would probably not be writing this book today!

For the next year, my life would be peaceful. I was working pretty steady. My grades had picked up, and I was in a steady relationship. Her name was Tanya Zachery. I met her in the lobby of the dormitory on campus, Creswell Hall. It was something about her. She just looked so humble and peaceful. We spent a lot of time together, and I can truly say that my wild side laid dormant. Tanya and I began to spend a lot of time together. I would pick her up from school and we would eat dinner and study at my place. Once I got back from work, I would take her to school before going to work at my other jobs. I loved her and everything about her. She was not like the rest. She was humble, trusting, and not into partying like the other women I encountered. I fell in love with her and wanted to be around her all the time. I was still reporting to the probation office from my first arrest on campus. Tanya would ride with me as I reported in. When Tanya went home for the weekends to visit her family, I felt lonely and sick. Of course, I was hard at work. I usually tried to work double shifts, not to think about the loneliness. Although we felt very deeply for each other, I didn't think either one of us was thinking about the next step. We were young and had our whole lives ahead of us. Tanya was focused on her degree, and I was focused on becoming rich and famous. Later on, our paths would take us in different directions.

High School graduation photo of Tanya
Zachery (Benjamin Graham's wife).

I was doing a great job at marketing my music. Here again is that determined kid to make his dreams come true. With all the jobs I had, I still found time to market myself. When I finished a shift at the radio station, I would spend another hour or two putting up posters in the different dormitories. I also put them on telephone poles around the city. This type of marketing made me seem bigger than life. Everywhere people went, they saw my posters. I was always willing to work hard and even sacrifice. In this case, I was sacrificing sleep, extra spending money, and hang-out time to build a foundation for my dreams. I decided to take my music to the next level. I formed a publishing company naming it Profitable Publishing Company and registered it with BMI. My first hit single was titled "Live the Dream." I played it during my shift at the radio station and put it in the stores in Athens. A few months after playing the song at the clubs, the main local radio station began to play it. I became famous at local level. I would be at the stoplight behind a car that would have a Benji K bumper sticker on the back, "Living the Dream." I always wanted to make positive music. I knew this from the first time I started to rap. Something inside me had an unconditional love for people and wanted the best for everyone. It was only when under the influence that I acted like a fool. Musical fame spread quickly through Athens and I began to do shows. One day, I got a call from the student activity center. They were putting on a show with De La Soul and wanted me to open up for them. I was so excited. I am about to meet the great De La Soul. When that night came, I rented a limo and arrived at the student center. The staff had reserved a dressing room for me. When my time came to perform, I gave a great show. Once the show was over, the members of De La Soul congratulated me on a good show. I did likewise and we parted. I partied the rest of the night with the limo drinking and flexing! I was again the talk of the town. A few more weeks later and another call came in. A major step show was going to be held at the Clark Central High School, and I would be the headliner. I was honored that people wanted to see me perform. The show was a huge success. The gym was full, and everyone was screaming for Benji K to rock the stage. What a feeling!

I also brought my brother down from Atlanta to be the DJ at the show. This was his first big show and he was excited. I believe this experience planted that music industry seed in my brother because after that show, he went on to pursue the music business as well. The newspapers decided to put me on their front page. Backing up a little, I want to add this to the record. When we reflect over our lives, based on our level of current wisdom, we can see where we went wrong. With all the fame I had and success I should have kept building, but after my best friend Spud quit college and came back to Atlanta, he was able to influence me to move to Atlanta so we could start a group. He and my brother rented this three-bedroom apartment where we would all stay and pursue our music careers. One of my major mistakes was leaving college to come to Atlanta, thinking I was going to blow up like I did in Athens. During the newspaper interview, I mentioned that I was leaving Athens to build my record label in Atlanta. The city was sad, but excited for me. I was going back to the big city to blow up! In 1990, I quit college and my five jobs to come to Atlanta with no real plan, but to blow up in the music!

CHAPTER 7

Back to Atlanta

It was the summer of 1990, and Benji K was headed for Atlanta. I just knew that my fame and fortune would pick up in Atlanta where I left off in Athens. Atlanta was too big for Benji K. Breaking into the music business was not as easy as it was in Athens. In Athens, I worked at the radio station. It was real easy to promote my own music. In Atlanta, I was not at the radio station and had to rely on the streets. I quickly became discouraged mainly due to the reality of having to find a job and pay bills. I was not happy with the change. In Athens, I was loved and everyone cheered me on. In Atlanta, no one cared and this depressed me. I began to drink heavily. I was averaging about a fifth of liquor every day. Getting drunk was no longer to party, but to numb the pain of failure. I took a few weeks to wallow in my pity and began to become determined again. I ended up saying goodbye to alcohol after I blew a potential job with AT&T. I had to go for testing and final interview, but the night before, I went out and got drunk. The hangover cause me to be late, and I failed my test. I realized at that point, alcohol would get in the way of my goals. I knew I needed to find work.

My brother and best friend had been carrying the bills and was starting to roll their eyes at me. I felt shame and went out to make it happen. I landed a job with a temporary service. I was great at data entry, so finding an assignment was easy. My first temp job was with the Dekalb County Tag office. I went through two weeks of training and was ready to work full-time. I turned out the be one of the best workers and eventually would be hired full-time. Working at an office with many people was good for me because I was able to get my hustle on. That entrepreneur side of me was always thinking of the next come-up plan. During this time, I sold merchandise from a catalogue. Our office held about hundred-plus employees and sales grew for my catalogue business. I saved on the shipping by driving to the warehouse and picking up my orders. My job didn't mind my extra income activity because I was one of the best employees there. I went above and beyond when it came to my work. Even the supervisors were ordering from my catalogue. Although I enjoyed the working, my desire was to be my own boss, to own my own business.

The catalogue sales were great but only because I worked in an office with many employees. I was afraid to leave because I would lose my customers as well, but something else happen. I met a friend who later became a mentor and business partner. Cecil was a real estate broker and was fascinated with my desire to be an entrepreneur. He gradually showed me how being stuck at the job and afraid to venture out was keeping me from living my dreams. I made the decision, and it was after being promoted full-time to Dekalb County Government Tax Office. I gave them my notice to leave. I was going to try my hand at the mail order business full-time. I decided to market singles membership ads through the mail. The name of my company was Graham National Communications. I set my numbers and began to go to work. The cost of an ad was $19.95. To respond to the ad was $2.00 per ad. This created a continued cash flow. My first issue had about 45 ads that were receiving many responses. My family was impressed. I brought the mail over one day to show them what I was doing. I let my little brother and sister, age 9 and 10, at the time open the mail, and they were amazed at the money coming in the mail. They found it hard to believe that people would put money in an envelope and mail it, but that's how mail order was at the time. Some paid by checks, but most paid by cash. Cecil saw that I built a successful mail order business and offered to help me take it to a corporate level. I would shut down Graham National

Communication, and we would incorporate a new company, Atlanta Social Network Inc. We would use similar concept, but would offer a singles membership, which allow the members to interact with each other. For $49.95, a person would become a member and be notified of events where we would bring the members together to meet each other and mingle. We made deals with movie theaters, pizza shops, bars, and more. We often would get bonuses for bringing crowds in these places.

Business was great. I was still working at the music as well, this time from a producer perspective. I was producing a guy named Rock Da Rula. Rock was also a heavyweight drug dealer in Decatur, Georgia. I knew nothing about drugs and didn't care for them. All I wanted to do was make music, and Rock loved the music I made. Rock would pay for the studio time, and we would go in a make a potential hit. Rock never would put the necessary money behind the single to get it out there, but he was happy bumping the CD in his car. We had fun at what we were doing with the music. We even did some shows together. These times excited me because it gave me a chance to get back on my music like I did at UGA, but with his presence demanded in the street and my presence demanded in the office, we had little time to build those musical careers.

As our business grew, Cecil and I financed a condo in the heart of Buckhead, the upper class section of Atlanta, Georgia. We went out every night on the town, bar after bar, partying, and treating each night like the weekend. We had a pretty good run with this company, but we didn't prepare for technical advancements in the market. We were solely a mail order business, so as the internet became more popular, we lost our market. Today as I look back, I should have converted the business online like everyone else, but we were too busy partying to realize what was about to happen. Before we knew it, sales dropped tremendously, and we eventually had to close our mailbox. Now keep in mind that I was living an upscale type lifestyle, in the heart of Buckhead being respected and loved by the family as a success story. How could I lose all this? I wasn't going to let that happen.

CHAPTER 8

Life Crucial Mistake
A Deal with the Devil

*Now when the people saw that Moses delayed to come
down from the mountain, the people assembled about Aaron
and said to him, "Come, make us a god who will go before
us; as for this Moses, the man who brought us up from the
land of Egypt, we do not know what has become of him."
Aaron said to them, "Tear off the gold rings which are in
the ears of your wives, your sons, and your daughters, and
bring them to me." Then all the people tore off the gold rings
which were in their ears and brought them to Aaron. He
took this from their hand, and fashioned it with a graving
tool and made it into a molten calf; and they said, "This
is your god, O Israel, who brought you up from the land of
Egypt." (Exodus 32:1-4)*

Sometimes in life, when we think that God is taking too long,
we began to make gods for ourselves.

Although we are able to bounce back from our mistakes,
they can be so painful. Rather than learn the ways of the internet
and grow with the times, I sought out the clients I was producing.
Why? Well, one night while I was leaving a bar, a guy approached
me about buying this expensive watch for only $10. I knew the guy

had to be on drugs. So being the inquisitive entrepreneur that I am, I asked him were there a lot more people in the neighborhood that did drugs. He said that there were. I told him I'm going to let him keep the watch and I was also giving him $10 to show me where these people were. He took me there, and I introduced myself to the people that were all living in this apartment. It was about eight people, and they all did drugs. I told them that I would bring some drugs from Decatur for them to sample and they could tell me what they thought. Can you imagine even making this kind of terrible mistake? I still went at it like I was a businessman. I left the house and immediately called Rock.

"Rock, man guess what? I just found a house full of smokers in Buckhead, and they all want to get some dope. Teach me how to sell dope so I can make some money."

Rock said, "I thought your business was doing good. Why would you want to jump in this game?"

I told him that I was going out of business, and if I didn't do something, I would be losing my condo as well. It took him a while to think on this, but I headed over to his spot the next day and did some more begging for him to let me in his drug business. Finally, he decided he would give me a try. He cut up twenty bags of crack valued at $10 each and told me that for every ten bags I sold, I would make $20 dollars. I agreed to our terms and tuck the bag a crack in my pocket and headed back to Buckhead. I arrived at the apartment and I was right on time. The people inside were waiting on their usual guy to deliver the crack to them. They had been waiting twenty minutes and were upset. I walked in and said, "Are you ready for some Decatur dope?"

One guy said yes. I gave him a sample and he went wild. The whole room lined up to buy my crack from Decatur. I sold out in thirty minutes. I called Rock and told him I'm on the way to get some more. After selling out three times in one night, Rock decided it was time to teach me how to cut my own dope. He went over the measurements with me. Each quarter weights seven grams. Twenty-eight grams to an ounce, etc. My cost was $250 for a quarter ounce.

I would cut up $20-size rocks and usually ended up totaling around $600. My first week selling dope, and I was selling 3 quarters per day. Earning $1,800/ day, netting $1,050. I have always been a hard worker, so I took this game and ran with it.

Cecil was not happy to hear what I had decided to do with my life. He was really disappointed and cut all ties. He said that if I got caught selling drugs or they found drugs in the condo, we would lose it and his license would be revoked as a real estate broker. He didn't want to take a chance associating himself with me anymore. I understood his point, but the money was too good for me to give up like that. We parted ways after that. I really felt bad letting Cecil down like that because he really saw potential in me, but my lack of maturity kept me blinded to the fact that the streets would be my downfall.

Rock and I talked.

"K man (He called me K, short for Benji K), you need to get you a spot of your own out there. Them smokers gone keep smoking up your profits. If you got to pay the house every time you make a sale, you gone lose money. Get your own apartment and put the workers in there and pay them instead some greedy house person."

I took Rock's advice. I went apartment hunting in Buckhead and found a two-bedroom apartment on Matheson Drive. I went in, paid the deposit, and signed a year's lease. I was in business! I had the utilities cut on and started putting together a crew to work that apartment. I had one guy to sell the drugs for me, another guy to answer the door, and another to deliver to the nearby houses in the neighborhood. By this time, I had built up a reputation and had phone customers that lived in Buckhead and along Roswell Road. I would deliver the drugs in a rental car. Now Buckhead was not exactly a mixed racial area at this time. If you were black and lived in Buckhead, you either played sports, acted in movies, or was a successful businessman. I chose the successful businessman look, wearing a shirt and tie every day to look less suspicious. Every day, I dressed for work in a shirt and tie with a leather trench coat on and went out to sell my drugs. I changed rental cars every three days to draw less attention to my running back in forth. Sales grew to $9,000 per week as my customer based increased. My area included Buckhead, Roswell Road, and Midtown. Customers preferred to deal with me because I didn't look like your everyday dope dealer. I was well dressed, spoke intelligently, able to conceal the real reason behind my visit to their jobs, homes, and public places.

For a few months, I felt like I was on top of the world. The money really began to change me. I became more arrogant and felt invincible. What I didn't know is that after a month a selling drugs and traffic coming to the apartment, I was under investigation. Not only had I put the first crack house in Buckhead, but I also rented XXX movies from that same apartment. People were coming from everywhere to rent adult movies or buy drugs. Neither customer questioned the other for their reason of being there.

Three months from the time I opened up this apartment to sell drugs and rent porn, the narcotics division of Atlanta kicked my door in. I can even remember passing the very cops that were coming for me. They were huddled up in a parking lot up the street from the apartment. I got on the phone and called to the apartment to warn the guys to be careful, there were an unusual amount of cops in the neighborhood. They were actually waiting on me to arrive. I rarely spent time in the apartment unless I was delivering more drugs to sell and collecting the earnings for the day. The Atlanta police obtained a No Knock Search Warrant which means they coming to search for drugs, and they're not knocking before coming in!

Around 12:06 a.m., I arrived at the apartment in went into the back bedroom to count the money. My foot was itching, so I took my shoe off and was in the middle of a good "scratching my toes" session when I heard this loud boom. It was the front door coming off the hinges. I heard, "Don't move, search warrant, get down!"

Within seconds of the police kicking that door in, they kicked in my bedroom door in. I had no time to react. The desk I was sitting at was turned over as the cop reached out to slam me to the floor. Money went flying everywhere. It was if they had been in there before and knew exactly where to go. I found out later that they had actually came in the apartment earlier that day claiming to be maintenance checking for roof leaks. They were actually getting the layout of the apartment. This was explained to me by one of my workers while we were in the back of the police van. He claimed he knew one of the cops from earlier that day. I scolded him for not letting me know that strangers had been in the apartment. I learn some valuable lessons that night. I knew what I was doing was wrong, but I didn't think the cops would come at me with such force. They even stayed in the apartment for another hour, locking up people coming to buy drugs. The acted like they were working for me, and as soon as my customers purchased drugs, they were arrested.

It would be weeks before I would be granted a bond to get out of jail. The judge finally gave me a bond, and I bonded out. I was worried about what the outcome of this case would be, but not worried enough to stop dealing drugs. I was bitten by the fast-money bug, and it would take a lot to get me off the streets. I contacted my customers and apologize for the interruption and told them I was still in business. I gave up the apartment, but would work off my pager. If they needed drugs, they were to page me and put the amount at the end of the number, so I would know exactly how much they wanted. It only took two weeks to build back up the money they took from me at the drug bust. I'm back on top and working harder to move up the drug-dealing ladder. I had met someone before my arrest that was considering fronting me keys of cocaine, but after the trouble, they wanted nothing to do with me. They couldn't trust my situation and didn't want to take the risk that I was working for the feds. I continued to go about my day selling drugs and networking to find my customers. I never reopened the apartment.

That small period of time spent in jail got me thinking about my previous skills as an entrepreneur. The social network that Cecil and I had along with other legit things I was successful at. I decided to lease a 700-square foot office space to start a legitimate company. This company would be similar to what I set up before. It was meant to develop into a local newspaper. I had a contractor come in and build a greeting counter. I purchased office furniture and hired my friend from high school to work there. All this funded of course with the drug money. My hopes were that the business would began to make money and I would be able to stop selling drugs, but the expenses from the office kept growing, requiring me to sell even more drugs to keep the doors open. Rock eventually dropped by and offered to help me pay the rent. I agreed and my vision for a legitimate business quickly became an office front for selling drugs. Rock would have his customers meet him at the office and would weigh the drugs up there. Who would have suspected we were selling ounces of cocaine out of an office building? After a few months of dealing from the office, Rock became a bit paranoid and eventually decided to get an apartment nearby leaving me with office to myself.

CHAPTER 9

The Birth of Addiction

After a year of selling drugs, something happened. I somehow didn't feel right about the idea. I never really felt okay about what I was doing, but now it seem to be a void in my life. I had VIP memberships at every club you can think of in Atlanta. I enjoyed the attention I got from this, but that too was getting old. I began to become depressed, simply going through the motions of selling drugs. I began to frequent the strip clubs more, seeking out paid attention from the dancers. I even made a few connections with the ones that wanted to buy drugs from me. We developed a regular routine. At 2:00 a.m., I would show up at the club, hang for about an hour, and then follow a couple dancers to their apartment where they would buy the drugs from me. They had this thing about tasting the drug to see if it were strong and then they would buy more. I quickly bought into this because I wanted to sell more drugs. After a month of this routine, I was invited to hang around for a while and watch the party. It was hard to actually grasp at first. My perception of everyone that did drugs was that they all was crackheads and ugly, but these dancers were far from that. As a matter of fact, most of my customers didn't look strung out. It looked like the dancers were having fun with the drugs. I was invited to try crack with them, "join the party," sort of. I took a few minutes to argue this suggestion in my head. I know how desperate people are on drugs. Why would I even consider this act? Between the sexual advances of the dancers and my arrogant belief that I would never be weak enough to be strung out, I dove in head first. One of the dancer's placed a $20-sized piece of crack on top of some ashes covering an aluminum can and put it up to my lips. She gave me instructions on how to inhale the smoke. She flicked the lighter and began to melt the rock on top of the can. She told me to keep inhaling and don't stop. She placed my hands on her hips while I was inhaling. She told me told hold the smoke for a few seconds and then release. My heart was pounding, and I felt this ultimate rush as if I had an orgasm. What in the world was this? This is awesome. I never felt anything like this before. I sat for a few minutes and repeated the process. I spent the night with them and smoked a whole ounce of crack.

The next day, I felt so depressed. How could I have done such a foolish thing. I was embarrassed. I felt insecure and worried about whether people would know that I had smoked crack. I soon snapped out of my pity party and got back to my normal day of selling drugs. A few weeks went by and the desire to try it again came over me heavy. I had a female customer that lived in a condo near my apartment. She would call me several times in a day for drugs. Her calls would come at late as 3:00 a.m. She called me and I went to deliver the drugs to her. I asked her could I chill out for a minute at her place while she got high. She agreed. She got high using a different method as the dancers. She had this long glass stem that she would put piece of crack rock on the end and melt it on to the screen at the end of the glass stem. She would then inhale the smoke and blow it out. I told her to let me try it with her. She didn't know that I had tried it before, but since this meant some free drugs for her, she quickly agreed. This went on for six hours. We smoked the rest of the drugs I had left over from the day. I knew I had money to buy more the following day, so I had myself another party.

My next days were always full of guilt and shame, but the guilt and shame got smaller as my parties became more frequent. Little did I know I was quickly becoming a junkie. It got to the point where I would get a hotel room away from everyone that I knew so that I could get high. My phone would be ringing with people wanting to spend hundreds on drugs, but I wouldn't answer because I was smoking the drugs myself. My habit grew to an amazing $18,000 per month. Sounds like a lot, but that is about $600 per day. The only way I could do this much was to sell and smoke. My drug sales amounted to $1,000 day so I began to smoke out at the end of the day. This discipline allowed me the ability to fund my habit. Eventually, this too would end because I was getting high more and more each day. My relationship with Rock began to become strained because he suspected something wasn't right. I got to the point where I couldn't afford my own drugs and would ask him to front me three and a half ounces to get back on my feet. My intentions were to stop, but as soon as I would get the drugs, I would have my own private party. Rock eventually cut me off.

"K man, you smoking! Look at you. You done got skinny. Something ain't right. I been doing this too long not to notice a smoker when I see one. I can't front you nothing else."

I told him I would get it together, but I never did. After Rock cut me off, I began to visit Boulevard in search for someone that would sell me quarter ounces. My customers would be nice enough to prepay for their drugs, and I would run downtown and buy wholesale, keeping the extra drugs for myself. I was still riding around in a rental car, but my progressed addiction cause me to lose that rental car. I couldn't afford to pay. I once rode for about two months until they found the car in an apartment complex and towed it. Because I had started smoking with my customers, I was able to use their desire to get high to allow them to trust me to get the drugs for them and allow me to stay with them while we all got high. They were too afraid to go downtown to buy drugs.

My weight dropped from 200 pounds to 130 pounds. I looked ill. I was so skinny. One day while riding with one of my customers, we pulled up to a traffic light near Georgia Tech. My mother was on her lunch break and crossing the street. I called out to her. She didn't recognize me at first, but when she walked up to the car, she had this look that I will never forget. It was one of shock followed by hurt. She started crying and ask me to step out the car. She knew exactly what I had been doing. She made a call to her boss and told him she had an emergency and would be taking the rest of the day off. She told me to come stay with her to get myself together. I agreed. I was tired of the cycle. I needed to rest and gain my strength back. I was ashamed of what my younger siblings would think. They remembered their big brother as the smartest man in the world. They remember opening envelopes with money in it. They remember me taking them to the mall to buy gifts for them. Now I was coming home a crack addict.

My younger brother and sister was staring at me as Mom and I walked through the door. Keep in mind that my family had not seen me for over a year. I had been too caught up in the drug dealing and smoking crack to contact them in person. I would talk over the phone trying to hide my situation, but was too ashamed to visit. Now the truth was out in the open. I told them that I had been messing up and needed to heal. They were relieved to know that I wasn't dead and understood my coming home. I slept and ate for two days. Mom had given me the upstairs office in her house. She had become an insurance agent and transformed the extra room in the house into an office. A few weeks went by and I was starting to feel pretty good. There were weights on the back porch. I began to work out. In the first month, I gained about fifteen pounds from eating, sleeping, and working out. Mom and I had a talk about what I wanted to do. I told her I want to go to work. She took me shopping and bought professional attire. I created a resume and started job hunting. After about a week of job hunting, I managed to get a temporary assignment through a staffing agency. It was a job for data entry, which was something I was good at. The assignment was to last only two weeks, but the owner loved the way I work and offered to hire me himself. I was so excited to be back on the right track. I told my mom the good news and everyone was happy. During this time, while working, I began to listen to various self-help tapes determined to become that successful businessman again.

Several months went by. I was eventually able to buy a car. It was a great deal from my mom's boyfriend at the time. My mom and I also talked about my joining her in the insurance business. She had quit her full-time job with Georgia Tech and now was ready to sell life insurance full-time. I joined the business with her while keeping my full-time job. It felt great to finally be on a pleasant level with my mom. She was not happy that I had chosen to sell drugs and she was extremely unhappy that I had gotten hooked on them. Mom was starting to trust me again. I signed up to sell insurance with a company. I'm not sure I was happy with the fact that my mom had quit her full-time job. I really believe that she should have stayed on her job until she built her business at a company. Mom was so excited that she just knew she would be making $100,000 plus in six months. I thought we would too, but network marketing isn't as easy as promoted. It is really up to the individual's drive, along with the rest of the team, that determines how far one will go. Mom struggled to the point of losing her car and having to file bankruptcy to protect her house. I was very upset with the people that promised my mom the stars, but we continued to work to build the business. Something I found out later in life was that one of my major triggers to use drugs was depression and setbacks.

Watching my mom lose everything depressed me. I counted it as a setback for us. I wanted so bad to be successful, but it seems like we were not doing too good. Depression grew worst, and I started to feel like I was missing something in the streets. One Friday night after cashing my paycheck, I went cruising around the Boulevard area in Atlanta. I told myself that I was going to give selling drugs another chance.

"I can sell drugs without getting high" is what I told myself. I saw one of the females walking the streets and told her I was looking to buy a quarter ounce of crack. I told her I'm trying to make some money. I would pay her to find me some customers and to hook me up with the weight man. A weight man is one who sold drugs in large quantities for the guys that often worked the corner. She introduced me to Stacy. Stacy was a guy that had an apartment on Jackson Street. He sold crack in all types of weights. Small stuff for the smokers or working sizes for the dealers. I bought a quarter ounce and left out the apartment. The girl told me about this lady that stayed next door to Stacy. She was a smoker and let people come in to sell crack and I could make some money there, so I followed her to this lady's apartment. *Knock, knock!*

"Who is it?" said Let, the lady who lived in this apartment.

"It's Star. Open the door."

Let opened the door, took one look at me, and slammed the door. Star banged on the door and told her that I was cool. She also told her that I had something for her if she would let us come in. The door was opened immediately. I went in and was told to have a seat on the sofa. Another young lady was sitting their smoking crack. I sat down and broke a $20 piece of crack off the quarter and gave it to Let.

Let took a hit and said, "You the man! This is some good dope."

The young lady sitting on the sofa asked me if I would sell her a dime of that dope. I asked Let if it was okay and she said, "You can stay the whole night. I ain't letting no more dealers in tonight."

The reason she didn't let me in the first time was that she thought I was the police. I was clean cut and looking well built. I sat for hours while people came a bought dope from me. It got to be late like 2:00 a.m. when it was slowing up. Let went in the bedroom and put on her nightgown. The other young lady stood up and started hugging her and something in me awakened. This brought back the memory of my first encounter with crack. It was about to happen all over again. I motioned for one of the girls to give me their crack pipe and I took a hit. That first one was so amazing. I felt another rush and began to get excited. The two ladies and I smoke up all my dope, and we spent the money I had earned earlier. It was about seven o'clock in the morning, and neither one of us was sleepy. We all were still wanting another hit, so I got in my car and went to the ATM. I withdrew everything I had saved while staying with mom. We smoked from seven that morning until about eight that night. At the end of this two-day party, I felt like crap. It is amazing how the real questions come to you after the fact. How could I do something so stupid? I know how tricky crack can be. I know the damage it does and how once started you never want to quit. Why did I restart?

What would I tell my mother? My family would be mad at me. All these thoughts took turn torturing me on the way home. Somehow, I was able to get myself together and make up a lie for Mom; however once I got to the house, Mom was out on a date, and the kids were asleep. I crept in the house, went into my bedroom, and collapsed into a deep sleep. Remember, I hadn't had any sleep in two days!

The next day, I felt guilty, but at least, I didn't have the jones of wanting another hit. I got up, ate, and went and lay back down. Luckily, I had another day to rest before going to work. While walking around the house, I pretended that I was coming down with a cold to hide the change in my composure and confidence. Something about drugs sucks the confidence out of me. As long as I am clean and moving forward, I can be confident, but when I am controlled by something so powerful as crack, I feel weak and afraid of what people are thinking or doing. Later as Mom and I talked, I told her I didn't come home because I had a new girlfriend and we were hanging out, that she had her own place, and I really liked her. Mom seemed happy, but a little suspicious of the story. I added to the story of going out a few nights in a role to account for the sudden drop in my finances. I thought to myself that I had overcame a big relapse. No one that mattered to me knew that I had tried crack again. This would be my little secret; besides, it was over. I wasn't going back that way any time soon. I quickly got back into my recovery routine, working out, eating, and playing big brother to my young siblings. One thing I realized is that one can never live up to their full potential covering up secrets or pretending to be okay when they're not. I became that person. I would pretend that I was that millionaire to be when in fact I was becoming a full-time crackhead. My routines to the crack house became more and more frequent. My thoughts became more and more irrational. I loved the attention I got when I arrived. People loved to see me coming. I usually would give everyone in the house a piece of crack when I arrived. Everyone in the crack house would call me the man and then put me out when the money ran out. Some of the crack houses would be nice about it because they knew I would return with some more money.

Mom began to notice a change in my pattern and decided to have a talk with me.

"Ben, I know it is not easy what you have been through, but you have got to stay focused and make something out of your life. You are losing weight and beginning to look like you did when you were doing drugs. You're not doing those drugs again, are you? No, Momma, I would never go back to that lifestyle. That's stupid and for quitters, and I'm not giving up."

Mom would look at me with that "I know you're lying look, but I just hope you catch on before it's too late." Finally, the obvious started happening. My weekly trips to the crack house became every other day. I found myself gone more than I was home. My promises around the house began to go unfulfilled. I was responsible for buying food since I ate the most. I did a great job of it until my addiction was active again. I would promise to go grocery shopping when I got paid. Mom was struggling already with the insurance business and really needed me. When payday came, I would get high instead. I ended up home on that Sunday night hungry and embarrassed for not keeping my world. My brother and sister began to argue with me. They called me a bum and said I was using Mom. The sad part was they were right. My addiction made me selfish. I thought about no one but myself. Ashamed of what I was doing, I would make a sandwich and go sit in the bathroom and eat. I didn't want them to see me eating food I promised to buy but didn't.

My job began to notice a change in my work performance and attendance. Sometimes, I would get high all night and be too tired to go to work, so I would call in. Eventually, the job decided to let me go. They were disappointed in me because I worked so hard until the addiction progressed, causing the decline in my performance. I managed to keep my drug habit a secret and led the job to believe I had become ill and needed medical care. They left the doors open for my return, if I got better, but of course better never came. It only got worse. Without a full-time paycheck, managing a full-time addiction would take me places I didn't want to go. I began to take things out the house. I can remember several occasions of being confronted by my brother and sister for missing music CDs and clothes. My brother was always on top of the clothes game, so he had the latest Polo shirts. I began to wear his clothes to look fresh when I went downtown only to take them off later and sell them to the dope man. I began to take his video games with me and sell them as well. I really hurt my brother behind this powerful addiction. I would always justify the act by saying that I would replace it one day. My financial obligations with my mom began to fall apart as well. I told her that the job laid me off and I would have to find more work, but after two months of not working and still being gone all the time, Mom began to worry and decided to have that talk with me again. This time, the talk was more direct.

"Ben, it is not fair that you stay out in the streets doing whatever you want to, then come home and eat up all the food without putting a dime back in this house. This has to stop or you need to move in with that girlfriend you keep talking about."

I knew it was time to stop dragging my family through the mud with my addiction. Once again, I stopped using drugs and began to move forward with my life. This lasted for about two months. Sales started to increase with my mom and me in the insurance business. We were doing well. Had a few people under us in our network and we all had great plans. I built up a little savings and was planning on moving into my own apartment. Mom was proud to see that I was finally making progress. I finally moved into a two-bedroom apartment on Martin Luther King Jr. drive. I was working a temporary assignment as a closer at a mortgage company. I enjoyed this assignment and did a great job. Mom was so proud that I had moved out the house and was living as a responsible individual. Once again, I got back in the routine of listening to self-help tapes and going to church. I told myself that maybe this time, I would go all the way and become a successful businessman.

A couple of months went by and I was celebrating my birthday. After work, I bought a fifth of liquor and went home to my apartment to drink and celebrate my birthday. I knew that I had moved to a rough area where I could easily buy drugs. Tonight I was feeling good and wanting to celebrate not only by drinking, but I was wanting to try some crack again. I had my own apartment. No one in my family would know. I could keep it my own little secret. I strolled out my apartment and stopped the first dope boy I saw. I bought $50 worth of crack and a crack pipe from the local store. I ran home excited to be celebrating my birthday. I prepared the crack pipe by inserting the wire into the head of the glass stem. I broke off a piece of the rock and began to smoke. I nearly choked myself! It wasn't crack. It was soap. I was so anxious to buy drugs I didn't think to check it before I bought it. I was pissed! No worries though. I just walked back up the hill and took my time until I saw what I considered a real drug dealer. This guy was parked in his car and other junkies were walking to and from his car. I knew he had to be selling good stuff. I approached and he stopped me in my tracks.

"Who you, man?" he said as he reached for his pistol.

"I live in these apartments. Just moved in and want to celebrate my birthday. I'm good. I normally don't smoke, but tonight, I am celebrating."

He looked and one of the other dealers chimed in, "He good. Tiger just flexed him for $50 and bought the real stuff from you."

The dealer reached into his sack and gave me a 50 dollar slab and a few extra sacks to make up for the rip-off I had just encountered.

"Don't mess with nobody but me if you want the good stuff," he mentioned as he gave me his number. For the rest of the night and most of that next day, I would call his phone up until I ran out of money. At the end of this party, I became depressed. I relapsed in the name of my birthday! This party lasted all night, and when it was time for me to go to work, I was purchasing more crack. I called the job and told them I was sick. I smoked all day until I had no more money in my savings or pockets. Finally, I went to sleep only to wake up the next day, not feeling like going to work. This time, my job was not happy and told me not to worry about coming back. Now the regretful thoughts started to dominate. Why did I do it again? I'm so stupid. I don't want nothing! I wish I was dead! The thoughts went on all day as I lay around the house, trying to figure out what to do in order to make sure my rent was paid. I finally approached the owner and told him my dilemma. He said that he needed a painter to help paint the vacant apartments. I was good at painting, so it worked out. He was so pleased with my work ethic that he made sure that I only painted the apartments. The other two maintenance guys were allowed to do other things like plumbing and electrical. We three became close with each other because all of us smoked crack. We would get together at the end of the day or either on our lunch break. We tried to keep it a secret from the owner, but he knew anyway. He was okay with it because we saved him a lot of money. He gave us somewhere to stay and a few dollars at the end of the day, we gave him a full day of keeping the apartments in good shape. This type of routine would go on for months before I would get fed up with being treated so harshly and looked upon as nothing because I used drugs. I was also exposed to the harsh violence of the streets. I was living on Martin Luther King Jr. Drive in Southwest Atlanta. I heard a comedian once make a statement about why are all of the Martin Luther King Jr. streets the most violent streets in the city? Funny, but so true. Every day, there were gun shots coming from somewhere in the area. Whether it was over a gambling dispute, territorial disputes, or just plain feeling disrespected, somebody always got shot each week. Once while getting high in the apartment from the upstairs window, I observed a man arguing with another man about being flexed. Flexed is when someone sells you fake dope like maybe soap or candle wax. This person sold the guy $100 worth of soap and the guy came back pretty mad. At first, the guy was denying it, telling him to get out his face, but the victim pulled out a gun and shot him in the side. His attitude quickly went from aggressive to "I'm sorry, man, here you go," trying to return the hundred dollars to the gunman.

The gunman took the hundred dollars and responded, "Man, you should not have flexed me in the first place!" He then shot him again this time in the chest and the guy that did the flexing collapsed onto the cement.

He lay there, screaming, "Oh, God, someone help me. He shot me. He shot me. Someone please help me!"

A few seconds late, he lay his head back and blood came up through his nostrils and out of his mouth. He was dead. To witness this hit me in such a way that I knew it was time for change. I was literally a few yards from all this. It was not a pretty sight. I decided I would get out of the routine of working to get high and try to find some other way. The owner made it clear that if I wouldn't work for him I would have to pay my rent on the first of the month. I was so determined, I agreed and went job hunting. I felt I wasn't well enough for office work so I resorted to day labor-type jobs until I could build my health and confidence back up. The owner was nice enough to break down rent payments in order to help me. He did understand that I was trying to get off drugs and was happy of that. He allowed me to pay him $125 per week.

In order to immediately get paid, I discovered the day labor method of working. That is when you go to an office and sit around hoping to go out to work that day, and when you did, you would get paid as soon as you got back in. The first day I applied, I was chosen to work on the back of a garbage truck. I was so excited to get the opportunity, I worked my hardest at this job. The driver was so impressed that he requested that I be the same worker for his truck the rest of the week. Once again, I was working steady. I credit my success to recommitting myself to spiritual growth. I began to study the Bible and pray. My routine became a positive way of life. I started my mornings usually with prayer and a good breakfast. I arrived early at the job to read my Bible. Others around me were talking about last night's parties and who got shot. I stayed focused on my Bible and preparing for the route of the day. The owner didn't mind that I wasn't working for him on a steady basis. He even offered me extra paint jobs and paid me as a contractor. It was very clear that he didn't respect workers that did drugs. Once I stopped using drugs, he paid me what I was worth to paint his units on the weekends. So during the week, I slung garbage as a garbage man, and on the weekends, I painted apartments. Once again, I experienced that feeling of being stable. This feeling would only last for about two months before I would self-destruct. It seems that I had a subconscious fear of success. As soon as things were going good for me, I would find a way to mess it up.

One weekend, I was to paint an apartment while the other two maintenance men were doing the plumbing and electrical. This was a last-minute job because that apartment would be rented out soon. Shawn, the apartment owner, wanted us to work overnight to get it ready. It was about 2:00 a.m. when the other two workers decided to take a break, a crack break that is. I don't know what I was thinking, but a strange thought came over me and created a powerful craving. I tried every bit of three minutes to fight this craving before I was asking to use one of their crack pipes to take a hit. After my usual two-month clean run, I was back on the dope. We worked and smoked all night, and it wasn't thirty minutes after Shawn came in to pay us that he found out that I was smoking drugs again. He was disappointed, but not as disappointed as I was. Once again, I was back in the cycle of going to a day labor to make $40, only to come on and spend it on crack. This cycle lasted for several months.

CHAPTER 10

Life-Threatening Injury

One day while working on the back of the garbage truck which was my favorite job, by the way, something happened that would have an huge impact on my life. Before this day, I had an uneasy feeling about the safety of working from the back of the garbage truck. Certain drivers would prefer to back down a cul-de-sac instead of going down and turning around. I felt the need to bring this up in a safety meeting. One particular driver would ignore company safety rules and would back down long cul-de-sacs. Every time he did it, I got this weird feeling, and then finally one day, he was backing down a long cul-de-sac and there were tree-cutting dump trucks at the end. Three trucks surrounded the end of the curve. He only saw two trucks and was steady backing toward the third. I saw that he was about to crush me while I rode on the back and began to yell. He couldn't hear me and the truck was moving too fast for me to jump off. I might have ended up under one of the tires because he was backing at a slant. I was on the back side of the truck so I couldn't jump in the hopper (where we throw the trash). I screamed one final scream before he pinned me between the garbage truck and the dump truck. Upon impact, I heard my bones crush in the pelvis area. It sounded like walking in the woods and stepping on the branches lying on the ground. Once I heard the crushing of my bones, my bowels released and I passed out for a few seconds only to be awoken to this awful pain that wouldn't go away. I screamed and screamed, yelling, "Oh God! Help me!"

Sirens wailed as the ambulance sped to the rescue. I remember a lot a people staring at me while praying as the rescue unit attempted to get me on the stretcher. The supervisor showed up and fired the driver on the spot. Wouldn't even let him back in the truck.

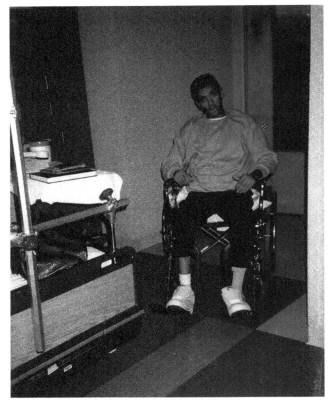

Hospital photos after a pelvis crushed injury.

I was rushed to Cobb Medical Center where they started emergency treatment. My brothers showed up to the hospital to access my condition. The doctors quickly got me sedated and gave me something for the pain. It was determined that I would need emergency surgery. I was transported to Lawrenceville where Mary Jo Albert performed an incredible surgery. She was able to put me back together again. I must make the point that it is the grace of God that allows us to recover and heal, but we also must thank God for the knowledge given to these doctors and surgeons that play a vital role in our healing. Due to my crushed pelvis, the surgeon had to insert a metal rod across my lower back. In my head, I was thinking that I would never walk again. Even after the surgery, the physical therapist would say, "All we can do is show you how to get into the wheelchair."

I spent months in intensive care. My attorney came to visit, and we prepared a suit against the company for their wrongdoing. My attorney told me that I would be looking at a great compensation for my injury. That news gave me a little hope as I lay in pain in the hospital bed. The IV needle attached to my arm would release morphine every few hours or so. Finally, after a few weeks, I started thinking about a new life. I knew that after the accident and being in the hospital for months, I didn't want any more drugs. I was expecting money from this, so I felt that I would get a new start and money to go with it. My spirits lifted. I had a friend of mine bring in some Cadillac brochures and the television in the hospital room stayed on the HGTV channel. I was looking at houses and cars. That is how I kept my sanity while healing. I also was studying the Bible again. The driver decided to pay me a visit. This was difficult because I warned him about backing down the street and he ignored me. I was very upset with him, but with him popping up, I was forced to forgive on the spot. Besides, what happened has happened and we couldn't rewind the clock. People make mistakes and those mistakes at times harm you one way or another, but after the harm is done, it is done. Forgive and move on to prevent losing peace over any of it. I remained in intensive care for another six weeks and was transferred to a rehabilitation center in East Point, Georgia.

My uncle Mack lived around the corner from the center. After two months of being in the hospital and spending the next few weeks in rehab, I thought it might be the right time to ask my uncle Mac, could I stay at his house while healing from the accident. He had an extra room that had once been used as a garage, but was closed in to create a family den. I never attempted to live with other family members while heavy on the drugs. I didn't want to drag them in my mess. Not only that, but I didn't want them always telling me that I know better and I am too smart to be getting high. I made a deal with my uncle that I would reimburse him rent once I got my unemployment and pending settlement. My uncle Mack was glad to see me and even more relieved to know that I didn't die from the accident. My uncle Mac always believed in me. He was all too familiar with addiction himself. A Vietnam veteran, Uncle Mac, came back from the war with a heroin addiction. The quality he required to supply his high would cost too much here in the United States because it was cut so much compared to the heroin in Vietnam. He decided to drop his heroin addiction and he succeeded. He confided in me that it wasn't easy, but assured me that determination would help me to overcome anything. Uncle Mac in his day was a wild one. His hangout was known as The Bottom in the West End of Atlanta. He drank and got high, but was also a revolutionary. My uncle was a Black Panther and hated what racism was doing to blacks during this era. The police were so abusive and violent that my uncle would just fight them because he knew they were going to attempt to abuse him.

My uncle eventually ended up in the federal prison system for forgery, but this still didn't keep my uncle from giving up on life. He obtained his education degree and once released from prison ended up working as a teacher in the Atlanta Public School System. How he did it, no one knows, but like I say, when you're meant to do something in life, good things happen for you. He told me that he never mentioned the prison sentence on his application, and it went through without an issue. My uncle is a perfect example of a convicted felon coming out with more value than he went in with. My uncle went on to become teacher of the year and was one of the best teachers in the school system.

Rehabilitation was painful, but I knew that it had to be done if I were to ever walk again. The physical therapist only taught me how to go from the bed to the wheelchair. The rest would essentially be up to me. Looking back at this injury, I feel that it could have went either way. Had I given up, I might still be in that chair, but I took getting my strength to walk again serious and gave it my all. Several months later, I became restless in that wheelchair. I started with attempting to stand up. At first, it was very painful, but within a few weeks, I was doing better. After a few months, I began to get the strength to take a step or two. Six months later, I was walking using the wheelchair as a walker. The restlessness got to me so I set my mind to do something around the house for my aunt and uncle. I actually painted their hall and bathroom while leaning on the wheelchair for support. I guess that was me, that kid that couldn't be still. Within another three months, I was walking slowly without the wheelchair. My recovery was remarkable; thanks to God and some determination. Another few months and I was walking normal, give or take a few limps here and there.

My uncle and I often talked of starting our own record label to produce positive music. We both agreed that someone needed to make music that was positive and inspiring. Our vision kept us excited. Early morning talks before my uncle headed off to teach were very enjoyable. We really came up with some great ideas. My uncle even decided to finance some equipment. I would pay my half once the settlement came in. We went to Guitar Center and selected the Roland XP80 along with some other recording equipment. Music has always been our family love and talent. Now would be my chance to create some awesome tracks for the world to enjoy. The next day while my uncle was at work I went to studying the equipment and by the time he got home, I had everything working and was already working on my first track. I count this as one of those happy moments in my life. I was off drugs and doing what I love to do: create music.

CHAPTER 11

Another Relapse

M onths went by and I was getting pretty good at making musical tracks. I submitted a few to a production company in Arizona and they loved them. As a matter of fact, they selected ten out of thirteen tracks. They mailed out a contract to me, and all I had to do was to send them the 24-bit copy of the tracks along with my notarized signature on the contract. This was great news, and it came right around my birthday. I had been stuck in the house for all these months, but now I am walking and ready to hit the streets and party! My plans were honest in the beginning. I just wanted to get out the house and celebrate my birthday. I bought some beer and began to drink. Feeling good. I bought another one and another one. Now I'm tipsy and traveling on Marta. Somehow, I had a bad feeling about my evening as if being warned by the Spirit that I would end up regretting the events of the evening, but I pressed on like a mouse nibbling on cheese in a mousetrap. I went back to my old neighborhood where they hadn't seen me since the accident. Bill and Larry were still working as maintenance men and was so excited to see me walking. I limped down to their apartment and sat down on the sofa. I had beer for everyone, and we were going to celebrate my birthday together. After twenty minutes of small talk, I began to ask for drugs. I asked if any one of them had a stem. They said yes and I sent them to get us some dope. My excuse? It's my birthday. I'll get back on track tomorrow I told myself. This relapse happened the same way all the others happen. Once again, I was back in the world of drug use. You would think that after all the pain and loss, that I would have learned my lesson, but addiction is cunning and baffling. My night ended with me smoking up all my savings to the point that I didn't even have bus fare to get back home. Luckily, Shawn had come in to work and gave me a couple of bucks to get back to my uncle's house. I would attempt to get back on track, but at least once a month, I would visit my friends and get high. This pattern lasted for a few months and then it happened. My lawyer called me into his office to accept the check for the offer he recommended me to take. What should have been $500,000 ended up being only $12,000 dollars. My lawyer told me that the insurance company were filing bankruptcy, and if I didn't settle, then I might not get anything. So I took the $12,000 and left. I owed my Uncle about $6,000 for back rent and my half of the studio equipment cost. I promised my other family members some money as well so I ended up with about $4,500. I ended up smoking for two weeks until I was flat broke. I really got upset about this because I dreamed of starting a new life with my settlement. I made an excuse to mess it all up because it wasn't the $500,000 as promised. That was stupid! I hated myself for what I did. I ended up back at my Uncle's house begging to stay until I figured out what to do with my life.

Fear thou not for I am with thee be not dismayed, for I am thy God I will strengthen thee. Yea. I will help thee. Yea. I will uphold thee with thy right hand of my righteousness. (Isaiah 41:10)

Landscaping Business

I think back to my various failures and realize that I was a stubborn soul refusing to totally give up on life. Despite my self-destructive ways, I would always try again and again. I never really wanted to accept the fact that addiction could keep me down. No matter how much damage my addiction did to my life, I would always keep the thought alive in my head that one day I would defeat it and live happy ever after. Today I realized that God kept me and watched over me throughout my struggles with addiction. He always made a way for me to move forward.

I arrived back home at my uncle's house, feeling defeated. I slept for a couple days and began to feel like myself again. I went into the backyard to think about my life and where I went wrong. How would I get back on track? The Spirit would give me the same answer every time. It is easy to get back on track. Stop using drugs. There is no heaven part of hell. You don't need it and you will never reach your goals as long as you continue to escape reality with drugs. I believed that every time I was comforted by the Spirit, my strength became renewed to the point I could come up with another plan to move forward in my life. Standing in the backyard, I began to look around. I was coming up with a new idea. I noticed a lawn mower, weed eater, wheelbarrow, and yard rake. That was it! I would began to make money by cutting yards in the neighborhood. East Point had a city ordinance that stated that all yards must be well kept or the occupant would be fined $90. This would bring me customers. I never thought about not having any money to start my landscaping business. I didn't have enough money for flyers, so I took my last dollar and bought a 100-page note pad for .69 cents at Big Lots. I wrote on each sheet of that pad, "Can I cut your grass? For the front yard, I charge …" and then I would put a line so that I could write in the price and leave the note on their door. I passed out all 100 flyers in the neighborhood. The very next day my phone rang. I had my first customer. I agreed to cut their front yard for $20. It took me fifteen minutes. They were happy and so was I. They wanted me to come back every two weeks! Within the next week, I had over twenty-four customers. Fifteen of those regulars (every two weeks). Soon the past mistake of wasting thousands on drugs was forgotten, and I was into the money again. I was making an average full-time wage by cutting grass.

I started this service in the spring during peak season. When it was starting to get cold, most of my customers were backing off. The grass wasn't growing as fast. I had to do something else. By this time, I had been clean for four months. Feeling confident, I decided to give the garbage truck a try again. I heard from a friend that Dream Sanitation was hiring helpers. I applied for the job and they hired me. My first full-time job with uniforms and benefits. I was excited. I told my uncle of the good news and told him I would love to rent the basement from them. I wanted to be around my uncle Mack. He was so wise and had been through the road of addiction. I really look up to Uncle Mac. We had great ideas and visions, so I figured that if I stayed there, we could make our dreams come true.

I was a little concerned about working on the garbage truck again. I didn't want to damage the rod in my back, but I felt great and in shape so I gave it a try. My first day was awesome. They were amazed at how good I was. I knocked an hour off the route my first day out. Things in my life was once again going good. For the next few months, I would work, come home, shower, eat, and enjoy a good movie. I felt normal. God always seemed to take care of me. After a few months on the job, I learned that the company was moving on Fulton Industrial Boulevard. The bus would go down there, but I would still have a half-mile walk to the warehouse after getting off the bus. I had not quite saved up enough for a car. I prayed that God would make a way. I didn't want to lose this job by being late. The earliest bus would get me there too late. The first week after the company moved, I made arrangements to ride with one of the drivers. He was known to call out so this worried me. My prayer was for a car.

"Father in Heaven, your servant needs a car to get to and from work. Please provide me with transportation. In Jesus's name I pray. Amen."

One day while on a route in College Park, I noticed a lady flagging us down before we past her house. I jumped off the truck to assist her with her garbage can. The driver hated when I did this because he literally wanted to pass them. I thought this was stupid because all she had to do was call the company, and we would have to turn around and come back. I ran down the driveway to pick up her garbage can. She was grateful. After returning the garbage can, I noticed a station wagon sitting in the yard. I asked her was it for sale and she asked me if I wanted it. I said yes and she said, "Come back after work, the keys and title will be under the seat."

I was excited. Can you believe it? A free car. Here I am praying and my prayer was answered with a free car to drive to work. My coworker gave me a ride back after work and we picked up the car. The story behind the car was that her husband who owned the car committed suicide. That car reminded her of him and she wanted it out of her yard. She was happy to get rid of the car and give it to me with no strings attached.

Blessings have followed me for as long as I can remember. I tell this story to everyone and give God the glory. The weather was warming up, and I would really do well this season with my landscaping because I had a car. I took one of my paychecks and bought some new equipment for the season. I loaded up my car and went to work. I could only work on the weekends because I worked full-time. I was able to pick up more customers because I could drive to them.

To this day, I can never understand why when things are going great for me, I tend to find a way to mess them up. After a few months of running my weekend lawn service and working full-time at Dream Sanitation, I began to get restless. My trips home included picking up a beer or two to take home with me to enjoy the movie. I rationalized that it wasn't crack and I was working hard. I deserve a beer when I get off work. My drinking increased. One day after pay day, I decided to cruise around the Cleveland Avenue area. I saw a lady walking down the street and offered her a ride. She immediately asked me if I wanted to date. I knew this terminology from back in the day from the prostitutes on Auburn Avenue. I told her no, but asked her if she knew of a place to go smoke crack. The thought came over me and I was off to the races. She took me to a lady named Linda on Third Street. They all thought I was the police until I took a hit of crack. Once I took that first hit, I knew I wasn't going home that night. I made up a lie and told my uncle Mack I was spending the night with a female friend to keep their worries down. A few hours later, I was broke and wanting another hit of dope. One of the dealers that was hanging at the house mentioned needing a ride. I gave him a ride to buy his supply from his contact and he paid me $5 cash and a $20 piece of crack. For the rest of the night, I would give people rides for crack. I finally got the strength to leave the trap to go home and rest for work. I would work until I got my next paycheck and go back over to Linda's house to get high. Eventually, this got the best of me because I ventured out one Sunday night and ended up having to call out sick at work.

My patterns changed at the job. My getting high increased, and my attendance at work became undependable to the drivers. They ended up firing me. I told my uncle they laid me off because they found out I had been hurt once before. My uncle listened, but something inside me knew that he knew what was going on with me. It was like he was a psychic or something. No matter how he felt, he really always gave me space to get myself together. This all came to a head one day when my uncle himself got drunk. He curse me out and told me I had to go. I couldn't believe it, my uncle was kicking me out the house. I knew I had to get myself together or I would be homeless on Cleveland Avenue. For the next few weeks, I would hang in the traps (crack houses or areas where drugs are sold) waiting to give people rides. I even joked about it, saying I was the trap taxi. At this point, I didn't even have my lawn service. I pawned all my equipment and had nothing but my car and the clothes on my back. My aunt boxed up what clothes I did have and kept them in the basement. For the next few months, I would sleep in my car and give people rides. My car ended up falling apart starting with the radiator fan. I had the fan sitting in the back seat. I had to stop ever few blocks to put water in the car. I had also received several tickets for riding without insurance and running stops signs. Nor did I renew my tag so they added that to my list of tickets. I kept on riding. Car running hot, tickets, nothing was stopping me from driving that car to make money for crack. One day after giving someone a ride, I was in a hurry to get back to the trap to smoke my rock they paid me with. I did not want to wait on any lights. I ran the first one. I kept looking in the mirror. I didn't see any police. So I ran the second one. My rock was sitting in the ashtray with my crack pipe beside it. I was in a hurry to get back where I could park and enjoy my hit of crack. By the time I ran the third light, I was pulled over and surrounded by four police cars. I panicked. I knew they were going to take me to jail. They jumped out the car so fast, I couldn't grab the crack rock or pipe out the ashtray. They pulled me out the car and handcuffed me. It so happens that while running all those lights, there was a detective on his lunch break. I was looking for police cars and didn't notice the detective behind me the whole time. That was it for my car. They impounded the car. The strangest things was with six cops looking over the car, not one of them thought to check that ashtray. When they allowed me to get my belongings out the car, I grabbed the rock and pipe without them noticing. Can you imagine the riskiness of all this? They simply wrote me some tickets and were going to let me go, and I still wanted to get that one rock and pipe out the car. Addiction can have us thinking so stupid at times. So now what. My car is gone. All the smokers that were jealous of my trap taxi hustle were laughing when I came back without a car.

"What you going to do now?" they asked.

I responded to them that I was a hustler and would always find a way.

I always noticed this labor place like the one I worked at before I got hurt. I decided to go in and apply for the labor pool. My plans were to work a day and buy a gram of crack and sell it to the other smokers. I did get a day's work in, and as soon as I cashed my check, I went to the dope man and bought a $25 gram. I cut it up into ten pieces value at $5 per piece. I sold out within an hour. I felt good about being able to sit and sell dope without smoking it up. I continued to work myself up to a nice amount and would then go back to Linda's house to smoke up all my dope. Now I was stuck, but a couple of the other dealers caught on to the fact that I could work a pack. So my next hustle began. They would front me 1.5 grams of crack. I had to bring them back $50, and I could keep and smoke the rest. This went on for a few weeks before I was finally arrested. One day while attempting to sell the drugs fronted to me, the Red Dogs, which was Atlanta Drug Task Force, jumped out the car, slammed me to the ground, and took me into custody. The charge was simple possession. I remained in jail for a few weeks. The judge decided to release me on a signature bond. After this happened, I decided to give the sober life another try. I reached out to a program and they accepted me. I told them about my pending court date, and they agreed to help me. The first thirty days was an in-house program and then I would attend group twice a week. I made it through my thirty days and began to feel normal again. So many times, I had been at this point. I was feeling great sober as if nothing bad was ever going to happen again. During this time, my uncle allowed me to stay with him while the program was getting an apartment ready for me. A few weeks later, I received the good news. The program's case manager found a one-bedroom apartment for me. My rent would be only $25 per month and the program would pay the rest. I was happy. Finally, I had made it. I was living independently without drugs. My uncle helped me move in. We gathered my things from the basement including my wheelchair. I had plans for that wheelchair. My uncle was proud of me. At this point, I got in touch with my mom. I had been avoiding her while running the streets. She was so disappointed in my activities. So many times before, I had told Mom I had it together, only to let her down, so I stopped contacting her. Finally, I felt convinced that life was going to go places for me. I made new friends at the apartment and participated in recovery-based activities. Life was good.

Benjamin took a wheelchair that he was once con-fined to and turned it into a snack cart.

CHAPTER 12

Birth of the Wheelchair
Big Mouth Ben

I began to think about how I could earn my money while in my apartment. I noticed my wheelchair in the corner. I took it out and placed an ice cooler in the seat. I then took a plastic tray that fit squarely on top of the cooler and created a mobile snack cart. I took $20 that I earned from cleaning a friend's carpet and bought a case of water and twenty packs of chips. I left my apartment and began to walk downtown. As soon as I got to Woodruff Park in downtown Atlanta, people began to ask me what I had. I told them water, soda, and chips. People lined up to buy their snacks. Wow! I sold out at the park. I pushed my wheelchair to CVS where I stocked up on more snacks. The first day I made $65. Excited about my new invention, I called my mom and told her. She was happy for me and expressed how proud of me she was. My new invention got a lot of attention from people. Nobody had actually seen a wheelchair used in such a manner. People talked, some positive others negative, but regardless, I kept going. My average earnings were about $75 daily. I began to save my money. I brought a new phone and ordered some business cards.

After a few weeks of pushing the wheelchair around, I came up with another idea. Why not put billboards on the sides of the chair and charge for advertising. This would increase my income! I went to the office supply store and bought material. I designed three sides, the right and left followed by the back wall. I created a name for myself, "Big Mouth Ben." My motto became, "If you want to sell it, let me tell it." The local businesses loved it. It took no time in filling up the billboards with advertising.

Things were going great for me. I began to notice that Auburn Avenue had a lot of club traffic on the weekends. I found out that I could make good money if I stayed out until the club closed. I tried it one night and made good money. People began to depend on me to be outside the club when they were leaving. My schedule on the weekend was to work during the day for a few hours, relax during the evening, and wake up around 1:00 a.m. to catch sales from the people leaving the nightclubs.

This plan went well for a while until I started to become depressed. I think that whenever life seemed to level off as far as progress was concern, I would become depressed. I experienced great feelings from the highs of life such as progress and new ideas coming to life. Whenever I wasn't creating anything, I would began to feel down. One late night while working the club traffic, I ran into a female that smoked crack. She lured me into some apartments with the promised of more business.

"There are a lot of people in those apartments on Fort Street looking for snacks," she said.

At first, I thought she was setting me up for a robbery. I wasn't afraid, so I went down that street. I knew that a lot of drug trafficking went on down there, but I didn't stop as if I knew what I was about to get into. I went to a few apartments and sold my snacks. The female invited me back to her apartment to meet her boyfriend and possible sell more snacks. As soon as I walked into the apartment, the smell of crack was obvious. My body began to shake. I knew that I shouldn't, but I believe that I made my mind up when I followed her down there. I sat down on the sofa and took a hit offered by another female sitting in the apartment. The initial effect was so great. It was like making up for all the time I went without it. I sat in that apartment and smoked morning until late in the day when I had no more money. Feeling ashamed, I left that apartment and headed back to my apartment. Once again, the questions arose. How could I do this again? I am so stupid. I don't want anything but to ruin my life. I crawled in bed and slept all night and most of the next day.

Monday rolled around, and I would try to live life again without drugs. I headed downtown and worked the crowds with the snacks on my wheelchair. I came home, watched a movie, and fell asleep. Things seem to be back to normal until the next weekend when I had a few dollars from the club sales in my pocket. I wandered down to Fort Street and knocked on Angel's and Mark's door.

"Who is it?" she said with a loud voice.

"It's me," I answered.

She opened the door and greeted me with a hug and invited me in. We smoked out again. Normally, my drugs wouldn't last that long because I had to give her and her boyfriend some. I didn't like how I felt after I would take a hit, so I would often smoke in the bathroom so that others couldn't see my reaction to the drugs after each hit. People in the apartment would often complain that I stayed in there too long. Finally, after getting harassed by the guest at the apartment, I left and went back to my apartment with the rest of the drugs. This was the first time I smoked crack in a drug-free apartment building. I was so nervous that they would smell the drug and kick my door down and put me out. I would burn incense to cover the smell. No matter how much I attempted to cover it up, I never felt safe. After every hit I would cover myself up under the covers, afraid of what may happen to me for smoking crack when I promised God I would stop.

My addiction began to progress. I starting smoking crack every day. I rationalized that my rent would be easy to come up with. Under a rental program I only had to pay $25 per month. I figured I could easily come up with this in one day, but as time caught up with me, I began to get behind on the rent, and as the months rolled by, I was in the process of losing my apartment. I reached out to my sister for her help. She came to the rescue. She wrote a check to the leasing office for the delinquent rent as well as a few months in advance. I was so relieved, but never stop getting high. I can remember so many times making empty promises to pay family members and close friends back. I had a pattern of letting people down including myself. As it turned out, my life became a consistent journey for drugs. I walked twenty-five miles or more every day selling my snacks only to spend it all on drugs. I became popular on Fort Street in Atlanta. Most of the drug dealers and smokers would buy snacks and cigarette lighters from me. I began to spend more time in the crack houses that in my own apartment. Most of the time, I would be in Mark's apartment. I would smoke until I had no more money and then push my wheelchair around selling snacks to come up with more money for drugs. Often, I would go overboard and find myself without money to buy more product to sell. I then would ask the store owners if I could clean up for a few dollars to stock my wheelchair. I learned window cleaning from my friend James, and it came in handy when I had no money for product. I set up a regular schedule with a Subway store next door to my apartment building. They would pay me to clean their windows every week. I would then take that money and buy product for my wheelchair.

CHAPTER 13

Homelessness

After several more months of getting high every day without paying rent, I was finally forced to leave my apartment. I had nowhere to go. I asked Mark if I could stay at his apartment until his girlfriend got out of jail. Angel had been arrested and was not at the apartment. Mark was a good person. He didn't want to see me out in the street, so he agreed. Now I am in the apartments of Fort Street next to all the crack houses. My pattern continued. I went out and sold my snacks only to come back and get high.

The Creation of the Snacks on Snacks Bike

Mark had a lot bike parts in back of the apartment. I got to thinking, I could get around a lot faster if I could put my snacks on the bike. I found a bike rack and put together a bicycle. I took some soda baskets and put them on the front of the bike. The basket in the front would hold my snacks such as chips, cookies, gum, and cigarette lighters. The cooler would sit on the back rack over the rear wheel. I was ready for a test run. The first run was unsuccessful. I didn't secure the baskets enough, and they fell off the bike. The people hanging out in front of the apartments all laugh when my snacks went everywhere. Some snatched them off the ground and ran while others attempted to help me. One of the drug dealers saw what happened and yelled at those that stole my snacks. He gave me $20 to restock my bike.

After a few adjustments, my bike was ready and I was rolling. I was so happy. I was still struggling with addiction, but I was content at the moment with having a way to support my habit. Once I could trust the bike for longer runs, I began to branch out. I would ride all over the city by getting on the Marta train and getting off at the stations and working those neighborhoods. People were fascinated with my creation. They called me Hustle Man. They really respected my way of making money. Word spread fast as people saw me riding all over town. One of the drug dealers came up with a proposition. He offered to give me a pack (bag of nickel-sized rocks) to sell for him. He told me I could keep one-thirds for myself. I jumped at this opportunity because I knew I could sell them easy to the other smokers that knew me. He gave me a chance. I was successful. I sold out in thirty minutes. He was impressed. I began to get a reputation for being a true hustler in spite of my crackhead habits. I felt good at first because I felt like I was successful at something although I was not able to get off the drugs. People respected me for who I was and I liked that.

Angel, Mark's girlfriend, finally returned home from jail. I was only able to stay another week before she began to get tired of me being around all the time. It just so happened that the guy I was selling drugs for was opening up his own apartment to sell drugs out of. He told me I could stay there. He sold drugs out of the apartment and let the smokers smoke in the kitchen. I would go out on my bike, selling my snacks along with his crack and come back in to take a break and return his money. It seemed to be a perfect plan for me. I wanted to get high, and now I had a pocket full of drugs to do so with as long as I kept his money right. Sometimes, I would go overboard, but would make up for it by hustling on the bike. I look back at these times and laugh at how hard I hustled. I can remember having no money to buy snacks for the bike. Once the dealer gave me work, I would sell a couple sacks and stock the bike up with it and make money off the snacks to replace his money. I had gotten so good at this, I began to flip everyone's money before I returned it. They would give me $20 to buy lunch from downtown. I would take $5 out of that $20 and buy a case of water, sell five bottles of water for a dollar each, and then return with their lunch and correct change. I would also get paid for going, usually a nick ($5 piece of crack). I began to love my lifestyle with no plans of getting off drugs. I began to look worst because I was always smoking crack and not eating. Some of the guys would look at me and say, "You ugly!"

I didn't care so long as I had my rock to smoke. At times, I was left to hustle for the dealer at the apartment. They would go to the club and leave me in charge of all the drugs and money until they got back. They knew I would keep things right for them. The thought being strung out always haunted me. That is why I tried to stay high. I didn't want to think of my current condition. I knew that life had to be better than this, but my addiction seemed so powerful and I had tried many times to stop with no success. I was beginning to accept life as it was and simply lived with the addiction rather than fight it. I found my confidence in my ability to hustle. People nicknamed me Hustle Man because of it. I took pride in that name. I enjoyed being trusted to do things for the drug dealers. They would all comment when things needed to get done and say, "Let Big Mouth Ben go downtown and pay your phone bill. You can trust him."

My errands for the dope dealers grew. They were soon trusting me to pay bills, pay the bonding companies, and put money on their friends' books when they were locked up.

As I was going through my struggle on Fort Street, I seemed to never forget that God was taking care of me. I knew whenever someone would find favor in me, it was because of God. I even had a chance to minister to the drug dealers in the late hours when they were going through their own problems. For some reason, they listened. I can count many times talking them out of committing murder when they fell out with someone or someone owed them money. The streets became a little strange to me. Although I looked at myself as trash, everyone that I worked for or did errands for seemed to respect me. They marveled at my humbleness and honest personality; well, at least most of them. I still had the hateful kind that would threaten me for no reason. Actually, I didn't always succeed at hustling.

One time, Big Boy fronted me a 1.5 gram of crack one late night. He said he would come back and collect the money the next day. I smoked up all of his dope with the help of a few people and fell asleep when it was all gone. My rationale was that I would go to work on the bike and make his $50 back. The worst thing happened though. I didn't wake up in time to go hustle his money back up. He woke me up, asking where was his money or dope. I lied to him, telling him that I left it in a bar I cleaned up at. I told him I was going to go get it just to make it out the apartment before he shot me. When I got outside, I got on my bike and left. I thought I would just make his money right quick, but nothing was happening good for me. The weather was lousy and it began to snow. It go so cold that no one was out downtown. Now I'm sleepy and starved and can't go back to that warm apartment because he was waiting for his money. I stayed on the run from him and went into a shelter. The next few days were terrible because there was a snowstorm. We were stuck inside. I began to get threatening texts from Big Boy. He said he was going to kill me when he found me. I wasn't worried about that though. He wasn't going to find me. The next day in the shelter, I became sick and had to go to the hospital. They treated me and gave me antibiotics for my infection.

Several days later, I started to feel better. I actually stay clean for a week by staying in the shelters and off the streets. Finally, the weather let up, and I was able to get back on my bike and hustle. I made his money and then I texted him. He gave me a meeting place and I took him his money. He still punched me in the face for taking so long, but I didn't care. I was ready for another hit of crack. I took the punishment in order to get high. One thing I learned from him is not to work for him no more. He was dangerous, and I wanted no part of him harassing me anymore. He tried to offer me more drugs to sell and I decline.

At times, I had a few issues with people in the street. They would mistake humbleness for being scary and used to call me scary.

I didn't mind them much because I knew the spiritual truth. You see, no matter what I went through, I knew that one day God would see me through. I learned that from the time I attempted to commit suicide. Although I knew this, I would still never give the sober life a determined try as I should. I was too quick to give up and return to the drugs.

Arrest photos of Benjamin Graham for possession of drugs.

After a few months of this ripping and running, luck started to play out for me. I began to get arrested. It was 1:00 a.m., and I was riding my bike with a pill bottle containing four crack rocks. I was trying to sell them to get my next pack. I was desperate because those last four sacks belong to the dealer, and if I wanted to smoke some more, I had to sell them. I rode my bike from one neighbor to another looking to make a sale. While coming down Edgewood, I passed a police car. He quickly made a U-Turn and pulled me over. He jumped out the car so fast I didn't have time to get rid of the crack in the pill bottle. When he searched me, he found them and placed me under arrest. I was nervous but relieved at the same time. Now I could get some rest. I knew that I would be in jail for a few months, so I sat back in the car and waited for the process to take place. At first, they tried to get me to talk about where the drugs came from. I knew better than to snitch on the person supplying me, so I made up a person and described him as if I knew what I was talking about. This time, they only charged me with possession. I was taken to Rice Street, which is Fulton County's jail for felonies. Now that I knew I wouldn't be smoking no time soon, I began to crave food. The trusty happened to be someone from Fort Street.

"Smokey, what up, man! Bigmouth, what you doing down here for. I see they finally locked you up. I told you to slow down on that bike."

I nodded with shame. I then asked him for a baloney sandwich. I was starting to feel starved. He quickly returned with two sandwiches on top of the two the guard gave me, and I chowed down as if it were steak. The whole booking process took eight hours before I was sent upstairs where I could lay in my bed. As soon as I lay down, I slept like baby. I was awakened by a female guard yelling, "Trays up."

It was breakfast and they were serving it at 5:30 in the morning. I was happy. More food. I made it through that day and was again awakened at 4:00 a.m. this time. It was to go to court. I was so nervous as to what the judge would say to me. They round us up and put us in a holding cell to await the bus that would transport us to court. The court time was at 9:00 a.m., but they put everyone downstairs early to make sure we all were there for court. The bus traveled from Rice Street to the Superior Court downtown Atlanta. I think it was another five hours before I was in the courtroom. I received the shock of my life when I went before the judge.

"Benjamin Graham, please stand."

I stood up.

"Due to lack of procedure from the officers, I am going to dismiss this case. You are free to go."

I was surprised, but excited.

"Once you get back to the jail, they will start the release procedures for you."

"Thank you, Your Honor," I said and returned to my seat.

Around two that morning, a voice came over the loudspeaker, "Graham! Pack it up."

This was it. I was going home. I gathered my items and headed for the door. Several hours later, I was released and given a one-way Marta pass. I headed back to the neighborhood. As soon as I got back, they were talking about the arrest. Of course, the dealers wanted to know if I said anything, but they knew the answer to that themselves. They knew I would never say anything. Later on that day, I went to pick up my bike from property. They kept my bike there when they arrested me. As soon as I got my bike, I was back in business. This time, I was going to try to just stick to the snacks. I stocked my bike and rode around for a few hours. I made the money that was owed to the dealer I was selling for when I got locked up. Instead of just taking the money and calling it even. He told me to keep it and instead gave me some more dope to sell for him. He also allowed me to live in the crack house. I tried to refuse, but he had given me some crack to smoke for myself, a welcome home gift, he called it. Once I got started, I knew there would be no stopping. I agreed to his terms. It wasn't two weeks before I was arrested again. This time, it was worst. I had just been given three grams of crack cut up into $5 nicks. As soon as I left the apartments, I was pulled over while on my bike. He immediately placed me in handcuffs and began to search the bike. He went right to my hiding spot, the handle bars. He found the drugs and began the testing process. Once confirmed, I was taken into custody. This happen right before the summer. This time, I spent about two months in jail. My court date got reset, so I was held in the jail until then. While in jail, I realized the stupidity of it all. While in jail, Atlanta was having record heat days with the weather. All I had to do was stick to selling my snacks. I could have been in the free world with my bottled water and still making money!

While in jail, I began to read my Bible. I became good friends with a guy that was being charged with murder. He and a guy got into an argument, and he pushed him. The guy fell and hit his head on a rock, which killed him. This guy that was charged with murder was a really good guy. Things just got out of control and ended badly. We began to study the word together. We even started prayer call before lock down at nights. At first, the inmates were reluctant, but little by little, they started to join us. My time passed peacefully while awaiting the next court date. This time, I was lucky. During the court date, the judge postponed the next court date and offered me a bond on my own signature. That means all I had to do was sign myself out of jail.

Finally, I was free again but not for long. I returned to the same apartment where I was working for the dealer. I really had good intentions of remaining drug free. I knew that word would get around that I was out so I made my way over to the apartment to speak with the dealer. The first thing he does is reward me with a gram of crack. Once he put it in my hands, my stomach started to turn. I couldn't fight the temptation. I went in the room with the other smokers and started smoking. After I took that first hit, I began to worry about what God was going to do to me. I had made promises never to return to crack. I vowed to come out and live a righteous life. I thought about how generous the dealer was and began to think it was a setup. I kneeled down on my knees in the corner and waited for God's wrath. A few minutes after calming down from that first hit. I began to take a second one. This time, I got the scare of my life. As soon as I took a hit, the dealer walked in the room with a gun. He pointed it at my head and yelled, "They told me you snitched, and that's how you got out!"

I am on my knees, begging for him not to shoot me and pleading my innocence with the streets.

"I would never do that!" I whispered back.

He said, "No! I heard this from an inside contact."

I really thought that my life was over. He continued to point the gun and he pulled the trigger.

I yelled, "Oh God," as I heard the hammer on the gun click.

He didn't have any bullets in it. He was joking with me all the time. Everyone in the room laughed at me. I was relieved but still shaking. I continued to smoke until all the crack was gone. He sat in the other room waiting as if he knew I was coming to ask for more. I went in the room and asked if he wanted me to work a pack. He said yes, and we were at it again.

With months of my release, I was arrested again. They decided to run the cases together and scheduled my court for late December. On the morning of the court date, I was so sure that they would just give me probation, I went about my day as usual smoking crack and running errands for the dope boys. My court time was 2:00 p.m. Around 1:30 p.m., I left the apartment telling everyone I would be back that evening. I arrived at the courtroom around 1:55 p.m. I sat through many cases. This judge was throwing the book at people. I began to worry about my cases. Surely, they wouldn't give me time. The prisons were crowded. I sat for a few more hours and then my public defender approached me.

"Mr. Graham, I want to explain to you the seriousness of your charges."

I panicked. The district attorney had took my past arrest in consideration and treated me as if I was a repeat drug offender. They wanted me to do ten years in prison! I told the public defender that I wasn't a drug dealer. I was addicted to crack and was caught with it only because I use it. She went over to the district attorney's desk and returned with another offer. They wanted me to take five years and serve two in prison. I thought about it. It would help me to get sober. I decided to accept it thinking that I would have one more time in the street before I turned myself in. The public defender mentioned that they would take me into custody that day. Once again, I panicked. I didn't want to go right to prison. I wanted to get high one more time. I pleaded with them to look upon my case as a struggling drug addict. They came up with another plan. They decided that if I pleaded guilty to the current charges they would give me a one-year program at Metro Day Report Center and five years on probation. I took that deal. Finally a program. I pleaded guilty to the charges and signed to paperwork.

"Mr. Graham, you are to report to the Metro Day Reporting Center in January."

I was pleased to hear this because it gave me two more weeks in the streets. The terms were firm, but I needed structure in order remain sober. I was to report every day to MADRC.

I left court and headed back to the apartments. It wasn't an hour after leaving court that I was back in the crack house smoking crack. This pattern went on up until the day I had to turn myself in. My intentions were to go, but when that day came, I didn't go. I knew a warrant would be placed for my arrest. I decided that they would have to catch me if they could.

My First Night Sleeping under a Bridge

The neighborhood started to change. Georgia State was buying up property, and the drug-infested apartments were part of that property. They gave everyone a thirty-day notice. I wasn't worried because I figured by that time, I would be ready to go in the program. When those thirty days arrived, the Georgia State Police started the check each unit to make sure everyone was gone. By this time, the drug dealers had moved out and the apartments were abandoned. Mark, the maintenance man, talked them into letting him and I stay on the property for another seven days. On that seventh day, I took two cushions from the abandoned apartment and headed up Fort Street to the bridge. People had slept under that bridge for years. I knew most of them. Marsha was one of them. I asked Marsha where I could lay my cushions down so I could sleep and she pointed me in the right direction. It seems that everyone under that bridge had two parking spaces each. This gave everyone their own privacy. Everyone minded their own business and were getting along with each other. I found a column and leaned my bike up against it. I chose the column so that it would hide me from passing traffic. I promised myself that I would go to the shelter the next morning.

The next morning when I woke up, I said to myself that it wasn't that bad. I once again put off going to get help with my addiction or turning myself in for the program mandated by the judge. I developed a routine of working the streets with my bike and then resting under the bridge at night beside the column. At this point, I was no longer selling drugs for the dope dealer. I stuck to my snacks. I also worked at the neighborhood convenience stores each day. One store, I would close out every night by stocking and cleaning. The other store, I did the same thing with the addition of landscaping the owner's house in Peachtree City. A few months had gone by since I failed to report to the probation department at MADRC. It was starting to get ruff for me in the streets. All I wanted to do was get high. I didn't want to feel anything. My addiction progressed, and I began to deteriorate. I barely ate anything. Each morning I woke up, I would eat an oatmeal pie, a bag of chips, and call that breakfast. I began to look very skinny. My face had sank in from the weight loss. I weighed about 140 pounds. That's skinny for a six foot four tall man.

"For I was hungry and you gave me food." (Mathew 25:35)

There is no doubt that God still loved and took care of me in the streets. People from various ministries reached out to me under the bridge. I felt embarrassed about getting in the line for food, but I knew I had to if I wanted to eat. I had also gotten to the point where I would not stocked my bike to keep the business going. I would sell my snacks and buy drugs. Each day, I woke up broke and had nothing on the bike to sell to make money. I also woke up with a heavy craving. Each day I had to either borrow $4 from the local businesses I did small jobs for or credit a 4 dollar rock from the drug dealers to completely wake my body up. In the streets, we called this a wake-up. Sometimes, I would be fortunate enough to run an errand for one of the dealers such as getting breakfast from local restaurants. They even trusted me enough to go pay their phone bills. These small trips kept me going as far as my addiction was concerned.

I think the worst part about my addiction was my ability to hustle and work hard. When all I wanted to do was get high, getting money to do so wasn't hard. I was willing to work for it or sell my snacks. My ability to get money would be the reason I would continue to remain strung out. My mind-set at the time was that I funded my own habit. There was nothing wrong with it. As the days grew, my addiction grew worst and worst. I didn't care about my appearance. People called me ugly and a junkie. I just smiled 'cause I knew it wouldn't be too long before my next hit of crack. I got to the point of wearing mismatched shoes. I didn't care what people thought. I wanted drugs more and more. I rode the bike for days before resting. My frustrations began to increase with using drugs, not because I didn't have the money. It was because I built up such a tolerance that the crack began to get weaker. They were cutting it more. I even began to taunt the dealers by saying that they were selling diet crack, cocaine-free!

CHAPTER 14

A Conversation with God
Surrender

When he came to his senses, he said, "How many of my father's hired servants have food to spare, and here I am starving to death! I will set out and go back to my father and say to him: Father, I have sinned against heaven and against you. I am no longer worthy to be called your son; make me like one of your hired servants." So he got up and went to his father.

But while he was still a long way off, his father saw him and was filled with compassion for him; he ran to his son, threw his arms around him and kissed him. (Luke 15:17-20)

Things began to change for me. My frustration began to allow me opportunity to assess where my life was heading. It didn't look good. I was already sleeping under a bridge, looking strung out. The businesses I did work for were starting to get tired of me begging for advances. It seems like even the dealers in the street were getting tired of my running. They started telling me I need to get help. You know something is wrong when a drug dealer tells you to get help. My normal opportunities were starting to dry up on me. My chase for the drug seemed to slow down. I accepted the fact that I would not get high like I used to. I eventually tried to drink more alcohol to help with the lack of real crack in the neighborhood. That didn't help either. I felt like God was telling me that my days of getting high were coming to an end. I felt that God Himself was preventing me from enjoying my high. I recall one time buying $20 of crack and putting the whole amount on my crack pipe. I took a hit and still didn't feel as high as I wanted to. I took that stem and broke it in disgust.

The next few days, the thoughts of a sober life were haunting me. I just couldn't seem to get rid of them. I spoke to God.

"There has got to be more to life than this!" As if God was sitting right beside me He spoke out in that little still voice, "It is. I promised to love you wherever you are. If you want to be under a bridge, I will love you there. If you want to go to prison, I will love you there, but it is up to you where you choose to be loved by me!"

It was like a light went on in my head. I felt my spirit lift a little. I became dizzy. It was at that moment I felt that my burden of addiction had been lifted. The Spirit was telling me that there was a big life waiting on me. All I had to do was sacrifice the crack. Let it go. Stop! I thought about this and that night as I lay on the concrete under the Fort Street bridge. I said, "Lord, I'm going to see how far I can go without smoking crack. I want to know what life holds for me. I know it has got to be better that what I have now."

That was my prayer and statement to the Lord before I went to sleep. The next day, I woke up feeling pretty good about life. I was going attempt to move forward without crack. Now whenever I make these decisions, it seems like there is a demon somewhere listening and that demon goes to work to make it easy as ever for me to get high. Later on that day while riding my bike near the Peachtree and Pine area, I noticed a sandwich bag on the ground next to a car. That bag was full of crack. Some dealer dropped his bomb (pack of crack) getting out the car. I didn't recognize who car it was, but I seized the opportunity. I picked up the bag and rode off. I wasn't sure how much it was, but I knew it was enough. My thought pattern went from wanting to get sober to wanting to get high. My rationale was this would be enough to get me high. I rode back to my spot under the bridge. I had about thirty minutes before I had to close up the Food Mart store. I took a hit and began to worry that someone saw me pick up this bag. Maybe the dealers would be looking for me. I became so nervous after that first hit that I didn't smoke another one. I said I would come back to it after closing the store. I showed up on time and began to clean up the store. I was rushing. I wanted to get back to my personal smoke party. I hid the crack in my blanket and tucked it neatly against the column. We had a code under the bridge. No one would mess with the others things. We watched out for each other belongings. So after I took out the trash, I swept and mopped the floor. I was standing outside the store waiting on the floor the dry when a gentleman called me across the street. He had a plate for me. I motioned to him that I didn't want it, but he insisted. I walked across the street to retrieve the plate, and as I did, a police car whipped up on the sidewalk and two police officers jumped out the car. I was calm because I knew that I didn't have the drugs on me. He called me up to the car and asked what I was doing. I told him that the gentleman is trying to feed me while I was working at the store. The police officer asked for my ID and went to his car. A few minutes later, he returned.

"Put your hands behind your back!"

My heart sank.

"What's wrong, Officer?" I asked.

"We have a felony warrant for your arrest out of Fulton County," he screamed as he was handcuffing me and placing me in the back seat.

All I could think of was that I would miss my personal crack party I had planned for myself. Also who would be the lucky person to find all this dope while I'm locked up? Curly was the officer's nickname. We gave him that when he first showed up on the block as a patrol. I had run-ins with him before, but this time, he had me and there was no letting go. Sitting in the back seat of the police car, I starting thinking about my conversation with God and how I wanted to see how far I go without dope in my life. I guess I was about to get my chance.

CHAPTER 15

Metro Day Reporting Center
The Turnaround

P rocessing at the Fulton County Jail was awful. It would take almost two days to get booked and upstairs where I could get in the bed and rest until my court appearance. Hunger began to set in. I was pretty fortunate in the holding cells. The inmates didn't care too much for the oatmeal being served, so I was able to eat a few extra plates. I took time to call my brother to let him know that I was safe off the street. My family often worried about me. Today, they tell me they used to be relieved to know when I was locked up. I told my brother I would be there for a while and could he please send some money so that I could order snacks. He agreed to do so. I was mentally preparing to remain in jail for a while. It would be two weeks before I would go before the felony warrant judge. Once I was in court, the judge asked for explanation as to why I didn't go as ordered. I told him I didn't have bus fare. I knew I was lying, but I was hoping he would understand. He said, "Okay, I'm going to give you another chance at Metro Day Reporting Center."

I said, "Thank you, Your Honor."

I told him I had a bike and would ride my bike there, but he told me not to worry. I would remain in custody until the day I start at Metro. I would be bused there with the other prisoners. I was disappointed. I thought I would get a chance to get out of jail, but my fast talking didn't work this time. I was stuck! I wasn't scheduled to go to the Metro Day Report Center for another three weeks. Once I got back to my cell, I began to get accustomed to doing the time given. Court dates were always a possibility to go home, but when you had your date of release or date of transfer, there was no need to get excited until the day of.

Over the next several weeks in jail, I stayed to myself. I got back into the word of God and began to exercise. It was a slow process because my body was still going through withdrawals. I would attempt to start on an activity such as reading or exercise only to be shorten with that feeling of depression. My body was protesting. It wanted dope. I couldn't give it to my body, so it would aggravate me with unusual pains and fatigue. Finally, the morning came to be transferred to Metro Day.

"Graham! Pack it up. Let's go," screamed the officer.

I packed my belongings and headed for the door. We were buzzed out by the guard in the tower. We went into another room where I was handcuffed to other inmates. We travel to several floors picking up other inmates. Finally, we were loaded onto a Fulton County Sheriff van. Some of the faces in the van were familiar. I knew a lot of people from the street because I rode my bike through all the dope holes in the city. We all were on our way to the Metro Day Reporting Center.

The van pulled into a gated parking lot on Sylvan Road. I was immediately greeted with this big blue sign Department of Corrections. I had a bad feeling about this. I wasn't sure I could make it through this without getting arrested again. We were ushered off the bus still chained to each other and shackles were on our feet. We formed a line side by side and were escorted into the building. We were all commanded to remain quiet until the process was over. They began to call out names. We all answer to our name when it was called. After that our chains were removed and we were seated. The director of the center came out and gave us the rules and regulations. When I arrived, I still had on the mismatched shoes, I was arrested in. A case manager called me into her office.

"Mr. Graham, do you need help with any mental issues?"

"Yes, ma'am. I was diagnosed as major depressive disorder."

"Okay, where do you live?"

"Ma'am, I'm homeless as of now. They arrested me near the bridge I was sleeping under."

She made a few notes and asked a few more questions. She told me to have a seat until my name was called again. This time, I was called into Mrs. Russell's office. She was in charge of the mental health clients. I would be grouped with them during my program at Metro Day. Mrs. Russell asked me similar questions and then handed me a referral paper for The Gateway Center in Atlanta. I was familiar with it. I stayed there before for a few weeks. I was told to go see them, and once they placed me on a floor to come back the next day with that information. She also gave me free bus passes to get there. I was admitted to the pre-treatment program at Gateway Center. They gave me paperwork needed to get another ID. My ID was lost from the time of arrest. I had to really start all over with that. Step by step, I began to get things together. I called Mom and told her I was in this intense program. She nodded as always. I couldn't help but feel her doubt as I told her I was serious about staying clean this time. I knew this time, I couldn't talk to no one about it. I just had to do it.

"You, dear children, are from God and have overcome them, because the one who is in you is greater than the one who is in the world." (1 John 4:4)

The rules were very strict. We had to report every day from 8:00 a.m. to 5:00 p.m. We were required to go to two NA or AA meetings every week. We were drug tested twice a week, and if we came up dirty, it meant seven days or more in jail. Everyone complain as the rules were explain, but nevertheless, we had to adhere. We had a chance to go to lunch and some of the clients kept going. I knew what that meant, so I decided not to go before that judge again. I knew he would send me to prison for ten years if I continued to ignore his orders. Several weeks passed and I was starting to enjoy this new life. Although there was a lot of structure, I had this feeling that now would be my chance to go all the way as I had talked to God about earlier. I did everything that program asked of me. I completed all assignments and remained sober. I eventually went to the night phase. This was easier. We reported three times a week and was drug tested only once a week. I was still doing good.

While at gateway, I came up with the idea to start my snack bike up again. I knew I would do much better now because I was sober. I did some landscaping for a store owner, and he gave me a few dollars and a new bike that was in his storage. I attached a basket in the front and a milk crate to the back of the bike. I went out and brought my first load of snacks. I was a little nervous at first because I hadn't done this sober. The last time I was selling snacks on the bike, it was to buy drugs. At first, I was a bit shaky, but the hustle kicked in and I was doing well. The first day out I made a few dollars and bought some person hygiene items for my stay at the Gateway Center. They wouldn't allow me to bring my bike in the building, so I locked it up outside with a combination lock. I felt so good about my first day on the bike and not having to buy drugs with the money I made. I rewarded myself with a movie and prepared to rest for the next day. I was due at the program early so I sat the alarm for 6:00 a.m. I woke up at that time, showered, and got dressed. Around 7:00 a.m., I headed out the door skipping with the good vibe of victory. As I approached the bike rack outside the Gateway Center, I stopped in midstep. Someone had stolen my bike from the bike rack. Broken pieces of the combination lock were on the ground next to the rack my bike was once locked to. I was heartbroken. I had only $50 on me, and that was not enough to buy another bike. I rode the Marta bus to the Metro Day Reporting Center. I shared my grief with other clients, but I knew they wouldn't understand. I decided to call my mom during the lunch break. I had talked to her earlier about the program and how serious I was about making it.

"Mom?"

"Yes, baby, how you doing?"

"Not so well, Mom. Someone stole my bike from the Gateway Center. I had put baskets there to sell my snacks. I am so upset."

Mom listened and told me that everything was going to be all right. This conversation brought back some much needed affection for my mom and me. I actually cried about the situation. Mom decided to help. She said that she would wire $200 to buy a new bike and merchandise to sell as well. I was so relieved. I knew that in the past I had did so much to my mom that I felt she would never trust me again. I thought she would just think that I was calling her with another lie, but she listened and gave me a chance to keep moving forward.

Birth of the Yellow Duct-Taped Bike

After finishing my day's task at the Metro Day Reporting Center, I hurried over to Walmart to pick up the money my mom sent me. Once I signed for the money, I also purchased a new bike. I bought the necessary parts needed to attach baskets. While browsing the store, I had a chance to see how God turned a bad situation into a blessing. As I was looking for tape to secure parts of the baskets, I noticed this yellow duct tape. It had a fluorescent look as if it were glowing. There were several bright colors, but yellow was speaking to me. An idea came upon me. I would tape my entire bike including the wheels with bright yellow duct tape. By doing this, people would know that this was my bike, and it also sent a positive message. The yellow would represent the sunshine, a goal to brighten people's lives. I felt so sure of my journey to inspire others that all my marketing angles would be related to uplifting people. So there you have it, the yellow bike!

I convinced the floor manager to allow me to bring the bicycle in the building. I made a promise not to sell snacks in the building. I told him of the last bike that got stolen and he quickly agreed. I took my bicycle to the second floor where I was temporarily living until my case manager found housing for me. We had an open dorm which used to actually be a jail. It was the old pre-trail jail in Atlanta. I took

Photo of the famous Yellow Bike known throughout Atlanta—
the yellow represents the sunshine -to brightens people lives.

out the bags of bright yellow duct tape and began to go to work on the bike. First I mounted my baskets and then I began to decorate the bike. I started with the rims. It took three hours to complete this task, but when it was done, I had what would become famous in the streets of Atlanta, the yellow bike. I sat back and observed my work. I was pleased. I took a before and after picture of the bike and sent it home to Mom to show her what I had done. I'm not quite sure she was happy with the duct tape on a new bike, but after I explain the reasoning, she said it was ingenious. It was about 1:00 a.m. before I settled down and went to sleep. I couldn't wait to ride my new bike. I was like the six-year-old kid waiting for Christmas. The next day arrived and I prepared to venture out with the yellow bike. Everyone that saw it inside the building went wild. They said it was cool and hip. Once I got on the Marta train, several of the riders began to take photos of the bike. Later that day, after my duties at the program, I headed over to the library and made signs with "Big Mouth

Ben" and "Snacks on snacks on snacks!" I placed these signs on the front of the bike. I also purchased a "Come in we're open sign" on the front and the side of the bike. People loved it. They had never seen anything like it. Here was a regular bike covered in yellow duct tape with baskets in the front and a cooler in the back, along with business signs such as "Open." I knew from the first few days with the yellow bike that I came up with a creative idea. The community was loving it.

My case manager was successful in referring me to HOPE ATL who in turn helped me find housing at Making a Way Housing Inc. This was a housing service for those in recovery. By this time, I was six months clean and feeling good. The classes were helping me to change my addictive ways. I really started to believe that I could remain sober.

I really enjoyed my stay in Making a Way Housing. Having found my new sober life, I was excited to participate in the life skill classes and meetings. My housing arrangement was tolerable. My roommate was an elderly man by the name of Mr. Dupri. He shared a lot of his life story with me. We got along so well because we both loved to make money. Mr. Dupri told me about his prison sentence. What was amazing is that this man had been in prison for most of his life. He was convicted for robbery and murder and sentenced to three life sentences. The only reason he was able to eventually get paroled was because a group he joined while in prison. This group was an intense life-changing group and was able to change my room-mate from the person he was when he entered the prison. He told me of spending three years in solitary for stabbing another inmate that was threatening him and much more. I was so honored to meet and talk with this man because this was proof that God forgives and change people no matter what they have done or been through. As we continued talking about prison, he mentioned the abuse suffered by the young men that entered prison. He had witnessed rapes along with other violent acts. This explains my purpose for encouraging young people to do their best to stay on the right path. I know that prison is no place for a young kid.

After a few weeks, I began to develop a routine around the compound. That is what we called it. I had purchased a steel lock for my bike to make sure history didn't repeat itself. I kept it locked up right outside my apartment. I would leave in the morning to attend my treatment program, sell my snacks in the evening and come home around 8:00 p.m. and reward myself with dinner and a movie. I was beginning to enjoy this new life and confidence in the sober life I never thought I'd have. The staff at Making a Way was impressed with my snack bike. They called me a real hustler, which I heard a lot in my day. It's been in my blood since those bottles I collected at the age of six. Although it made me feel good to be complimented by the staff, I would was really impressed with the fact that I could remain sober and build the life I wanted in the first place. To add to my seriousness of recovery, I entered an online associate degree course in alcohol and drug counseling. I qualified for financial aid and took advantage of the educational opportunity. I enrolled and immediately started studying. I attended class daily via computer in the computer lab at Making a Way until my computer was shipped to me.

CHAPTER 16

Unexpected

The Metro Day Reporting Center was preparing us for graduation. I had met all the requirements. I completed my early recovery skills class, cognitive therapy, and community service. I was a year clean, and everyone was proud of me. The counselors came together and decided that I was one of those most improved clients in the program. They asked me if I would give a speech at the graduation. I was honored. Excited, I phoned home to Mom.

Benjamin Graham's mother.

"Momma, guess what? I have been selected to speak at the upcoming graduation. They were impressed with my activities and thought I would be a good candidate."

Mom was excited.

"Baby, that is great news. I'm not going to miss this. I will come down the weekend before and we can hang out. I am so proud of you. I always knew you could do it. One year clean! My baby!"

I felt so good. I had not been clean for longer than a few months in the whole seventeen-year struggle with addiction. I was happy.

Words can't describe the feeling I had during this time. As the time grew near, I stayed in touch with Mom to see what day she would come down. Mom had been through some things with her husband dying a few months earlier. I was happy that she would come down and hang with the family. Mom announced that she would come down on that following Thursday. Once she arrived, she chose to stay with her daughter, Mia. This was around her birthday, so I went out and bought flowers. I met her at the North Springs Marta train station. I couldn't wait to show her my bike in person.

"Wow, baby, you really have decorated this bike. It looks like a mobile store," Mom said as she examined the bike.

"Yeah, Mom, I chose yellow to represent the sunshine. I want to brighten people's lives. I want to be that example where people look at how my life turned around and they will have hope that things can happen for them too," I said with compassion.

We discussed the times for the graduation and parted. Later on that night, we all went out to dinner and had a wonderful time.

Making a Way was excited for my graduation too. They often bragged about how serious I was about living in recovery and refusing to return to active addiction. They rarely worried about my activities. As the weekend approached, I made plans to hustle hard because I wanted to make sure I had enough money to buy a suit for this event. I worked ten hours Friday selling my snacks. After I finished, I went downtown and purchased a suit. It had been years since I wore one. There was a time that shirt and ties was all I wore.

My goal was to be a millionaire by thirty and a billionaire by forty. As you can see, I fell a little short, but was back on the journey. I called Mom to tell her that I had gotten a suit. She offered to give me money, but I wanted to do this for myself. She did however mention that she was going to help me with my business license as a graduation present. I told her about my music and how I wanted to revive Profitable Publishing Company, which would make positive songs to uplift people. I formed this company while in college some twenty years ago. It was still registered with BMI. She loved the idea and agreed to help me with the license. Friday night, I watched a movie and went to sleep excited about the things that were unfolding.

7:00 Saturday morning, my phone rang. It was my sister, Mia. For some reason, I didn't feel right when I looked down at the number. I tried to think positive. Maybe she was making plans for Mom to come spend the day with me. Mom did mention she wanted to stay over at my apartment. I answered the phone.

"Hello?"

There was this frantic voice from my sister. "Ben, Mom had a heart attack, and we're heading to the hospital. Romero should be coming to pick you up in a few minutes."

My heart raced as my spirit sank. What happened? I just talked to Mom. Where did all this come from? I went into the front office in tears. I told them what happened and that I will be leaving with my brother. They said a prayer as my brother pulled up to the gate. I got in the car. We both were nervous. We did not expect this. All we could do was hope for the best. We made it to the hospital in thirty minutes. We met Mia and Henson, my other brother, at the emergency entrance. They showed us which room Mom was in. As I walked in, I was in total shock. Mom lay there unconscious, not responding. They had her on some machine assisting her with breathing. I held her hand and she moved a little. This gave me hope that she would be all right. Full of tears, I prayed and talked to Mom, telling her she would be okay. We spent a few hours at the hospital, waiting on her condition to get better. We all decided that we would meet back at the hospital the following day at 1:00 p.m. The doctor recommended that we give mom room to recover. The next day, we all met at the hospital. We spent a few hours in the waiting room waiting on the doctor to tell us what was going on.

"Heavenly Father, I know, Lord, that I have not lived my life the way I should in the past. I know I missed a lot of give years with my mother because of addiction. Please keep her here so that we can live and enjoy life together. In Jesus's name, Amen."

Finally, the doctor came out to talk to us. He told us that her condition had not gotten better. They would have to do surgery to stop the diabetes from spreading. I knew Mom had an issue with diabetes, but I didn't know it to be this bad. After the doctor left, we gathered and prayed asking God to heal mom and make this all better, but even after that, I didn't feel too sure. I began to get angry. Why was this happening to us? I knew with anger came other feelings that I wasn't prepared to deal with at the moment. I made a phone call to my sponsor. A sponsor in recovery is a person that has significant clean time and looks over others new to recovery. I told him my situation and how I felt. He recommended that I go to a meeting that night. I didn't want to because I didn't want to leave my mom, but after a few hours at the hospital, I got an urge and decided that it would be best to go to a meeting.

I often went to the NA recovery meetings every Sunday night. This was my home group, and I felt very welcome at this group. Tonight, I would have to share with the group that I was not as strong as I thought.

"Hello, my name is Ben and I'm a grateful recovering addict."

"Hey, Ben, welcome!" the group responded.

"I want to start off by saying that I'm afraid. My mom came down from North Carolina to see me speak at the graduation from a recovery program. She had a heart attack and is in the hospital. Her condition is bad, and I'm just a mess right now. I'm mad and feel powerless over the situation. I just need to voice this now in desire of support from you all as I go through this moment," I shared.

As soon as I said, "Thank you for letting me share," my phone rang. It was my brother.

He said in a very faint voice, "She didn't make it."

I can remember just yelling, "No, man, no, man," as I collapsed in the meeting. A few of the attendees escorted me outside and into the laundry room as I cried for what seems like hours. Even during this horrible moment, I didn't get high. I went home and went to sleep. I woke up the next day and starting crying all over again.

I told Metro Day Reporting Center of my loss. They consoled me and said they would leave an empty seat in the audience for her. I told them I would still speak in spite of the current situation. Most of my counselors suspected that this would be my time to relapse, but through the grace of God, I remained focused as graduation night approached. I gave my speech and it brought tears to everyone in the room. The staff at MADRC brought flowers to give me for my mom. All of the family came to support me this night. I was happy to see them there. My brother and I hugged at the end of the night, and he suggested that I really look into public speaking. I had done such a great job. He said I was a natural. Although it was a great night, I couldn't help but think of Mom. I felt so terrible. If I had gotten clean earlier, I could have spent some quality time with her. Maybe I could have prevented her health issues. All these things were running through my head as I went through about my usual activities. For a while, I felt guilty, but thanks to my life skill classes, I began to properly grieve the loss of my mom. The funeral was well done, and the family had one more chance to celebrate Mom's going home service.

Relapse Can Sometimes Happen!

A few months passed since my mom's death. I had gotten behind a little a school, but the teachers allowed me to take a leave from class because of the death in the family. As much as I knew of the right thing to do, I felt void as I went about my day. It was hard to shake the fact that Mom was gone. I shared a lot in the meetings and spoke with my sponsor about the situation. I tried to do as much as possible to move forward without my mom. I did well until Mother's Day approached. This was the final trigger. All the family had other family to celebrate Mother's Day with. All my brothers and sisters were trying their best to deal with this day the best way they could. I took a ride on the bus downtown. I was moving as if I had no control over my actions. I didn't even bring my bike. I had already made up in my mind what I was going to do. I called up an old friend that rented out rooms of his apartment. I told him I didn't want to be disturbed. I purchased $100 of crack and locked myself in this room. That first hit brought back instant memories of getting high. For the moment, I was in crack world. Feeling no pain but feeling the guilt behind my relapse or should I say slip. The drugs lasted for about three hours and I needed more. My friend didn't want me running in and out, so I told him I wasn't coming back. I went to the ATM and withdrew another $100. I was so depressed that I didn't even care no more. It was like I was trying to return to the bridge as fast as I could. I actually took the drugs and sat under the bridge with the other crack smokers and started smoking. News spread fast about this, and before you know, dealers and smokers who were proud of what I had done came to talk to me.

"Big Mouth Ben, what are you doing! Man, you were doing so good. You need to stop and just go home," said one of the dealers.

It was touching to see a drug dealer wanting me to get back on track more than wanting to make a sale. I told them why I was under the bridge smoking, and they left me alone, one by one. They just gave me space. Most of them still had their moms, so they couldn't imagine what I felt. Finally, the expected happen. It wasn't getting arrested but much worst. I ran out of money! I had no more money to buy crack. I talked one dealer in to crediting me more but after that it was really over. Dread, another friend of mine from the streets happen to walk under the bridge. He saw me sitting on this stone smoking and he freaked out.

"Big Mouth Ben, what the heck are you doing? These people aren't your friends. If they were, they would tell you to go home. I will walk you to the train station myself. Please let's get up and walk away from this. That's all you got to do is walk away and you can to your stable life."

His reaction and words were convincing; besides, I had no more money. I didn't even have bus fare to get back on the train. Dread walked me to the station and paid the fare for me take the bus back to Making a Way.

While sitting on the bus, I decided to work on recovering from this night in the street. I called my sponsor and told him what I did. I told him and my group friends I was on the way back to Making a Way. They said they would meet me there. Once I got back, I went into the office and confessed to what I had done. I wanted to be honest because I wanted to get back up. The office told me to go rest and they would talk with me later. They ended up placing a restriction on my movements for thirty days. My group members showed up at the apartment and just gave me this biggest hug to let me know it was going to be alright. They sat with me for an hour and then left. I slept most of the day and woke up feeling frustrated by what I had just done. It took a few months to get back to my confident recovery walk, but I made it. It just so happened that once I returned to class, one of the subjects were on relapse versus slips. The book mentioned that slips are when you give in to drug use but get back up and never returned to it. A relapse was returning to active addiction. I know I will get a lot a reaction to my theory concerning clean time, but this is how I view it. I slipped for a night, but the next day, I got back up and went back to my walk in recovery. I didn't lose any training taught to me by Metro Day Reporting Center or the life skill classes at Making a Way. All the knowledge about addiction didn't go away either. So who came up with this rule as if in a game that you had to start all over? Your mind doesn't start over, why should you? I picked up where I left off. I had to deal with a few consequences such as regaining the money lost, breaking the rules of Making a Way and the most painful one, self-defeat. In certain groups of recovery, there is a counting system. You pick up a white chip which means you coming out the rain. You get another color in thirty days, sixty days, and so on. Now it is a great thing because it motivates you as you strive to get more colorful chips, but what does it do to you when you slip? You had a one year chip and you went out one night and had a drink. Now as if in a game, you have to come back in the room and pick up a white chip as if your life is starting back over. Your life is not starting back over. You still have the same amount of recovery in your mind. The lessons are still there and a slip serves as one more lesson. Needless to say that I stopped counting my clean time. To me, counting your clean time is like seeing how many days you can go before you mess up again. This is no game! I don't need chips to tell me how clean I am. I simply know I am clean. There is really only two ways, clean and unclean. Everything in between is false confidence. I feel you really only have today clean. Recovery suggest we take life one day at a time so why not count it as one day at a time. Can a man say that he is four years clean? Where is it? Can he pull it out his pocket? Now although I see things a little different than the average guy in recovery, I do know that measuring your clean times keeps you focused and it is like a reward for achieving a certain period of time clean, but beware of this method and keep moving forward one day at a time. I did and things started to work out even better than I imagined.

As time progressed, I was nearing completion of my associate degree in counseling. I had continued on without another slip. I was determined to build this new life of sobriety. I worked harder than ever. I actually came up with a route for the snack bike. I ran this route the same way every day. I even ventured out to more areas using the Marta train to get around. I would ride my bike to the train station and take the train to the west end and work that area. People were starting to recognize this bike as being everywhere.

People often commented, "Man, you be everywhere!"

I smiled because I knew they were right. I went wherever I could go without problems. I also increased the number of accounts I had with my window cleaning service. My friend James taught me how to clean windows years ago and now it was coming in handy. At one point, I was cleaning one-third of the businesses on Auburn Avenue windows. I had an ongoing contract with Subway or Edgewood and also cleaned the pharmacy. I started to set goals for myself. I opened a bank account and committed to saving a certain amount of money each day.

CHAPTER 17

Back into the Music
Big Mouth Ben: Motivational Entertainer

I decided to spend a weekend with my brother, Henson. He wanted to show me how he was coming along with his beat machine that Mom and I bought for him a few years ago. I took the northbound train to Doraville station, locked my bike up at the bike rack, and waited on my brother to pick me up. Once he arrived, we loaded my snacks into his car and left the bike secure at the station. We made it to his house and started to listen to some beats. Henson was good. He was natural at music like Grandmother and others in our family. Music was one of the many talents that were given to our family. As we went through each of the beats, one of them caught my attention. It was a dance beat with a banging bass sound. I started singing to myself. All of sudden, I came up with a hook chorus to the beat.

"I got that monkey off my back, now I'm seeing stacks, selling my snacks like the hood sell crack."

Henson loved it. He put the beat on CD, and I took it back to Making a Way to write my verses to it. Hours later, I had a snacks on snacks song.

"They buying all my water, my candy for a quarter, If I ain't got it, I'll go and fill your order. Got snacks on snacks on snacks, got snacks on snacks on snacks!"

The next weekend, I went back to the studio and recorded my first song. It had been years since I had been in the studio. I was excited. I played it over and over. My brother Romero went over to Henson's place and mixed it for me. I was so happy! Now I would come up with an idea. Why not buy a radio with a boom sound and mount it on my bike? I purchased a big radio and mounted it on the front on bike. It was so loud that people thought it was a car with a booming system. I started riding around promoting my song. Within weeks, the neighborhood started reciting lyrics from the song. This inspired me even more to keep writing songs and recording. I got a few more beats from my brother and went to work. By the time I wrote my next song and was ready, my brother recommended that I go over to my cousin's house to record. He said that Mack had a better recording program and could mix it for me. I knew I had to pay for studio time even though my cousin was more than generous about recording. In recovery I developed a very good habit of showing support for people when they were putting in time to help me. I decided that I would pay for my studio time. Excitedly, I came up with a budgeting plan. I estimated to cost of each song to run about $400 after recording, mixing, and mastering. To accomplish this, I put aside $30 a day for about twelve to fourteen days. I came up with this by selling my snacks on the bike and cleaning windows on Auburn Avenue. After that, I would put my song together with the help of my brother and my cousin Mack who was also gifted in music and vocals. The people on the compound at Making a Way loved my songs. They just knew one day, they would hear them on the radio. I thought so too so I kept going. I decided that I would market my music like the big boys. I had flyers and posters made. People were starting to take me serious. My next song was "Relapse," story of a fall, which talked about my slip during Mother's Day. After that, I came up with another song, "Came from Nothing." My cousin sang the chorus to this one. Finally after a few more recordings, I had enough songs to create my first mix tape. It would be called Rap Motivation. I knew there were millions of people rapping, mostly young. Where would I fit in? Most people would consider me too old to be rapping. I came up with the concept used today. I created positive hip-hop to further brand myself as a motivational entertainer. What better way to reach the streets but through positive hip-hop? I knew that I had a huge journey ahead of me, but I kept going. I pressed up my first batch, a hundred compact discs, and sold them from my bike. I was able to recoup some of my cost from the sales. A few months later, I shot my first music video. It came out well and I kept going. Life was good, but I was starting to feel lonely. I prayed, asking God to send someone my way that I could enjoy the rest of my life with. At this point of my life, I wasn't interested in trial dating (three-month relationships). I knew I couldn't handle the roller coaster of emotions that came with that, so I remained patient and didn't rush into anything.

CHAPTER 18

My College Sweetheart

It was 9:30 p.m. as I was browsing the internet and social media marketing on Facebook, I came upon a profile that really made my night. It was Tanya Zachery, my college sweetheart. I mentioned her earlier. When I clicked on her photo, my heart pounded. It was her. Where had she been all these years. I often wondered what she was doing. I knew that she worked security for Georgia State, so I thought she might be a police officer or something. It turns out that Tanya had transferred her credits from the University of Georgia and completed her education at Georgia State University. She majored in science and was now working in her field. As I starred at her picture, I noticed something that never changed, those precious eyes. Something about her eyes always attracted me. She just looked so pure! I had to inbox her, see what else was going on in her life, and ask her on a date. I sent her an inbox message on Facebook. Tanya responded. She left her number. I couldn't wait to talk to her. I dialed the number, and it went into voicemail. I automatically started to talk myself out of it.

"Man, what would someone like that want with you? You are a recovering drug addict!"

Just as I was about to agree with myself the phone rang. It was Tanya. Her voice was so pretty. It was exciting to hear from her after twenty-four years. We set up a date at the Underground Atlanta.

When Tanya arrived and stepped out the car, I gave her a hug to make up for twenty-four years. I really missed her.

"Girl, you haven't changed a bit!" I said.

"Neither have you," she said, as if she couldn't breathe from that twenty-four-year squeeze I was putting on her. We headed inside Underground Atlanta to have a snack and catch up on the past events. I immediately went into full gear, revealing any and everything about myself as if I was attempting to sabotage her opinion of me. It wasn't that though. I was so into Tanya that I laid all of my past struggles on the table for her. I wanted her to know everything about me so she could decide that night whether she would want to see me again. I actually feared that she walked out on me. During the conversation, she asked to be excused to go to the ladies room. Those were the longest three minutes of my life! I thought that I had told her too much. Each minute she was in the ladies room, I was thinking that she was going out the back door. Finally she returned and I could breathe again. We enjoyed the rest of the night laughing and talking catching up on lost time. When I got home, I literally floated into my apartment. I was in love! It didn't take much to know that Tanya was the one for me. I had remained abstinent during my struggle with addiction. I wasn't really into casual sex. The only thing I wanted during my addiction was drugs. For the next few months, Tanya and I dated. We really enjoyed each other. It was like the time never went anywhere. We had picked up where we left off in college.

Life was really starting to look good for me. I developed a route on the bike for the snacks that included hair salons and barbershops. I even stopped off at certain apartments where the neighborhood would hang out. I was also building my client list for window cleaning. At one point, I was cleaning windows for half of the businesses on Auburn Avenue. Tanya and I were getting closer by the day. We just knew we were meant for each other. I didn't want anyone else but her. I made a decision. I was ready to propose! I prayed about it before going to sleep. I really wanted to spend the rest of my life with her. I went to sleep thinking about Tanya.

"Heavenly Father, I thank you for Tanya. I pray that she become a permanent part of my life. If it be your will."

The next morning, I received a call from my sister, Mia.

"Good morning, big brother. How you doing?" she greeted me with so much love. "You know I've been thinking about you and Tanya and I really had an idea. You know that I still have Mom's wedding ring and jewelry, and I think God is telling me to give it to you for Tanya."

My jaw dropped. I was witnessing the power of God. After my prayer with God, He led my sister to call me and offer these things. I was so grateful. Now I could propose to Tanya with a special engagement ring from my mom.

The plan was put in place. I invited Tanya out as if we were going to someone's event at Chateau Elan. My sister, brother, and his girlfriend were already at a suite inside Chateau Elan. We parked the car and met them in the lobby. We went upstairs for a bit and talked. The plan was for me to walk Tanya around for a minute while my sister prepared the room. She put pedals on the floor, lit several candles, and made a heart shape design on the bed. By the time we got back, they had everything ready. There was music playing. We entered the room. Tanya looked around amazed at what she was seeing and wondering what was going on. As we got in the room, I took the engagement ring out my pocked, got down on one knee, and asked Tanya to marry me. Several seconds went by which seem like hours. I was waiting on her response, but she was so taken in by the surprise, she didn't respond right away. Finally, I heard those words. Tanya responded with an emotional yes and the room cheered. I got to say, this was the best day of my life.

We had an awesome dinner near the winery and enjoyed a fabulous night at the hotel. The next day news about the engagement had spread all over social media. All my Facebook and Twitter friends were congratulating Tanya and me on the engagement. We both were ready for an exciting future together.

CHAPTER 19

Opening the Store

The next few months, I worked really hard at building a sales route for the bike and publishing music through Profitable Publishing Company. I had big plans for Tanya and me. I knew that we were meant for each other and God would bring some great things our way. While riding my bike on Auburn Avenue, I passed the very bridge I slept under as I always did because it was part of my route. As I proceeded down Auburn, I came across a For Rent sign in one of the shop windows near Wheat Street Baptist Church. I leaned the bike up against the building and took a look through the window. Inside the window, I saw this long narrow space. A vision came to me. I saw drink coolers to the right, a counter going across the back and shelves on the left side. I was visualizing a store! I thought about it and began to get excited. *This could work,* I thought. It would be right across the street from the senior citizen high rise and the historical Wheat Street Baptist Church. It was also near the King Center so tourist would have easy access to souvenirs and snacks. I dialed the number to make sure it had not been rented out. The broker said that it was still available. I told him that I would check with my wife and we would call him back. When I called Tanya and told her about the vacancy, she became excited too. Tanya had always saw me taking the snack bike to another level. She always believed that there were great things inside of me. She was very convincing too. I love her so much for this. Although the cliché mentions behind every great man is a woman, I like to correct that by saying beside every great man is a great woman. This was our chance.

I said, "Baby, they are asking for a month's deposit and first month's rent and the space is ours."

Of course, there was an application process. We met with the broker and looked at the space inside and out. We both were satisfied with it. We decided to go for it. We completed the application and was told they would get back in touch with us. Now I began to worry. Maybe my credit wasn't good enough. Maybe they would find out about my history of addiction and running up and down Auburn Avenue. Tanya stopped me in the mist of my stinking thinking.

"Baby, relax. We prayed to take this to the next level. God would not bring us this far only to have us turned away."

I agreed. Mrs. Robinson, the owner of the building, would be making the final decision, and as it turns out, she was led by the Spirit the whole time. She just felt it was the right thing to do, give us a chance to live out our dreams. She called us and told us to come pick up the key! Tanya and I brought a table and chair from the house to sit in the store while we mapped out the layout. Our layout was exactly like the vision I had while looking through the window.

" Take therefore no thought for the morrow: for the morrow shall take thought for the things of itself." (Mathew 6:34)

A few days into planning and I began to worry. Tanya had been assigned to work out of state for a few months as a consultant for a medical device company. At the time, she was the only licensed driver. I began to ask myself, "How would I get stock to the store?" "How would I get shelves and other items?" I also began to wonder about the rising cost of getting the store ready. I knew I would have to do most of the work myself such as painting. I brought in Mark, my old friend from Fort Street, who was a very talented handyman to build a back counter and help with other issues. Somehow, my passion outweighed the concerns because everything came together. I rode my bike to the nearest home improvement center, bought some paint and whatever else I could carry on the bike, and returned to our future store. I even talked to Mr. Holley, the convenience store owner on the other end of Auburn Avenue. I worked for him and learned mostly about a convenience store set up. He was excited for me. He helped out by lending me his old retail counters and candy racks. I had no truck to haul it back to our store, so I used his hand truck and walked the counters down Auburn Avenue. Cars were passing by me, staring as if I was still that strung-out individual trying to sell something. Some drivers even shook their head while others laugh at me walking down the street with an eight-foot counter. They didn't know I was taking that stuff to my future store. As we finished painting and organizing the counters the store still seemed to be missing wall shelves and middle isle type displays. I priced an eight-foot single wall unit and found out they wanted $169 for just one 2×8. It would cost me almost a $1,000 for just some shelves! I prayed and decided to wait on something else.

"Heavenly Father, please help me to put this store together. I know that You have blessed us with the opportunity. Forgive me for my worries and doubts but I need help."

A few days later, while riding my bike to the Marta Train Station, I observe this guy loading what appeared to be shelves unto his truck. From the looks of the truck and the metal on the back, I knew this guy was a recycler. I turned in the driveway and asked about the shelves. The guy was literally taking the brand-new shelves out of boxes to load on his truck for the scrap yard! He had at least 10 boxes of new 2×8 shelves like the ones I priced earlier. I asked him what he would charge me for those shelves and to deliver them to the store. We worked out a figure which came up to be about $200! Blessings! One hour later, he was parked in front of the store and we unloaded the shelves. Mark spent the next few hours putting them together. This was what we were missing and once again my prayer was answered. I had $1,000 worth of shelves in my store for only $200.

Tanya was due back in town, and I really was excited. I wanted to surprise her with the whole new store look. I only sent her photos of certain items but never the store after we had fixed it up. I wanted that to be witnessed in person. We drove to the store, and Tanya was very impressed. Now she was really excited. We spent the weekend dusting and cleaning the store. We also went to the wholesale warehouses buying stock for the store. Grand opening would be a few weeks away. Everything seemed to flow naturally as if meant to be. Even the licensing process went through without challenge. We opened a few weeks before the official grand opening. The neighborhood was loving it. The story spread quickly throughout the city. When people came into the store, they were amazed at what we did with just that small space. It looked neat and clean. What seem to come together so easy ended up ministering to many people. Here I was on Auburn Avenue, a street that I spent so many years strung out on drugs, homeless, and defeated. Many of the people on this street knew me from my struggles on Auburn, but today by the grace of God, I was now a business owner along with my lovely wife. From sleeping under a bridge to keys to my own store three blocks from that same bridge. It was apparent that God had blessed me. It was the point of surrendering and then the decision to move forward with stubborn determination. I choose the word *stubborn* because it describes my journey in life. I was that kid that had to touch the stove and get burnt before I believed that it was hot. Now I would use that stubbornness to succeed. I would move forward refusing to believe that I didn't deserve the good life I so much desired.

The first week we were open, several of my friends from the streets came in. Some became emotional at what they saw. They saw a real convenience store. They remembered the old Ben. They also remembered how hard I worked on that bike and they were extremely happy for me. The neighborhood supported us. We never had to worry about robberies or snatch and grabs. As a matter of fact, Tanya and I decided against installing bullet-proof shields like one sees when they walk into the other stores in the neighborhood. We wanted the customers to feel that warm welcome. As it turns out, we were right. Most of the customers responded at times that there was something special about that store. I politely confirmed their comment with a confident "Yes, it is. This store is anointed."

Grand opening went well. My family and Tanya's family showed up. We had a great time. The seniors across the street played games and danced to then music all day long. Auburn Avenue Specialty and Gifts was a hit in the neighborhood!

CHAPTER 20

The Wedding

As the months passed, business grew. It was slow, but we were growing. People were starting to find out about the little small store on Auburn. Tourist enjoyed their visits to our store and were very inspired by the love story of Tanya and I finding each other after twenty-four years and the story of my having gone from sleeping under a bridge on Auburn to owning a business on the same street. We found out quickly that a convenience store is hard work. We had to constantly stock the store. We didn't have many deliveries coming to the store. They mostly turned us down because they said we didn't have enough traffic. We had to shop and bring the stock in most of the time ourselves. We quickly found ourselves putting in fourteen-hour days with a forty-five-minute commute each way. One night, we were so tired after leaving the store, we forgot to lock the burglar bar door. All night, the door swung back and forth. No one even attempted to break in the store. When we arrived the next day, we saw the door open and thought someone had, but after reviewing the cameras, we saw that we never even locked the door! Regardless of the hard work, we were determined to make this store work; besides, we had a wedding to plan for.

Time was nearing and we began to lock down some times and dates. The wedding would be held at 103 West, a wedding venue on West Paces Ferry road. To me, this was symbolic because it was around the corner of where I once lived Pharr Road. Life was coming full circle, and I would have another chance at happy and successful living once again.

Benjamin and Tanya's wedding photos.

I chose my brother to be my best man. He was so excited for me. My brother had pretty much been there for me throughout my journey. We both dreamed together of having a record company one day. We published songs together and just knew one day we would make it big, but I disappointed him when I got into the drugs. He saw the rise and fall. It was him I called in the middle of the night while high on drugs, thinking I heard someone on the roof. He saw and felt the pain of a loved one suffering from addiction. Today, he was one happy person to know his older brother had overcome addiction and was on his way to being a happily married man. Everyone was excited and ready for this big day. Tanya and I worked day and night to make sure everything was planned smoothly. We scheduled a rehearsal the night before. The day of the rehearsal, we went out to start the car and it wouldn't start. I panicked and became upset. How could this be happening the day before the wedding! Tanya was the smooth one, and her smoothness rubbed off on me. Instead of complaining, we decided to handle it the way successful people would. We had it towed and repaired while we rented a car. This lesson would help me grow out of complaining when things came up or I experienced temporary setbacks. Setbacks will happen. It's how you deal with them that determines your outcome. Rehearsal went well, and everyone returned home to await the big day.

4:30 a.m. and I'm up. Too excited to sleep. I feel like a kid on Christmas. This was really going to happen. I was not only on the right path, but now, I would be on the path with the love of my life, my missing rib as so spiritually put. I began to cry thanking God for the biggest blessing of them all someone special to spend the rest of my life with. A few hours, I was able to go back to sleep. The morning of the big day, Tanya and her daughter Tanisha headed over to the venue. I spent the day handling business online and preparing for the special moment. My brother arrived to pick me up. I was already emotional.

"Don't start that!" my brother joked as he gave me a hug.

Understand that even today I cry. I am an emotional bean bag when it comes to my testimony. After having gone through what I have and to be where I'm at, I have a lot to cry about.

We arrived at 103 West. Tanya was in a private room, getting dressed. I wouldn't see her until she walked down the aisle. My brother and I went into another room, and he helped me prepare, making sure all my tuxedo buttons were attached and everything in line. A few minutes later, the ceremony began. The pastor entered first and waited at the podium. A few minutes later, I walked down the aisle and waited alongside my best man. Reggie and Akeem joined us as their counterparts lined up on the other side. As the music played, I witnessed my soon-to-be wife being escorted down the aisle by her father. I couldn't hold it in any longer. I cried as I watched her gracefully come down the aisle. She was so beautiful. She looked like an angel. Within minutes, we were going through our vows to one another. Thoughts ran through my head as if my whole life flashed before me. It was like God was showing me all the things I gone through to show me where I was at the moment. I cried some more.

This was the happiest moment in my life. We kissed and was pronounced man and wife. From that point on, we had a wonderful time celebrating with family and friends another happy moment. Several hours later, we loaded into the limo and headed to the Hotel in Buckhead. We would remain there until 6:00 a.m. We had an 8:00 a.m. flight from Atlanta to Miami. Our honeymoon was going to be a seven-day cruise. The cruise ship was leaving out of the port of Miami.

Saturday morning, August 23, 2015, we boarded the plane headed to Miami. We arrived in Miami and began the boarding process for the cruise ship. This would take several hours, but we didn't care we were on our honeymoon. Hours later, we were aboard the cruise ship. Our room was facing the ocean. This was awesome! I had never been on a ship before, and it included all you can eat, casinos, entertainment, and much more. We had a chance to visit Montego Bay and climb Dun Rivers Fall. We were able to tour Grand Cayman and other wonderful sites. Our honeymoon was an enjoyable six days of love and fun.

Nightmare on the Cruise Ship

It was Friday night, and we were enjoying our last night on the cruise ship. We would be back in the Miami port soon. About 3:00 a.m., the ship pulled in. Tanya and I were sound asleep when we were suddenly awaken by loud knocks at the door. There were several knocks, and then the door was opened by the ship's security and customs police. They flashed their flashlight in our faces and asked me to get up and put my clothes on. Once I was dressed, they asked me to step outside the room. They told me to verify my name with them. Once I did, they told me I had a felony fugitive warrant out of Atlanta, Georgia. My heart sank. How could this be happening to me and on my honeymoon at that? I told them there must be some mistake, but they didn't want to talk about it. They said I would have to take it up with Dade County Police when they came to get me. Tanya was very upset as she watched the police handcuff and take me away. I could only imagine what was going through her head. At first, I thought someone had put something in our bags, but it turned out that it was some warrant filed by a court in Atlanta. I remained in the holding cell for a few hours, and finally Dade County police showed up to escort me to the jail. By this time, it was 9:00 a.m., and people were everywhere outside the ship. I was so embarrassed walking past the families in handcuffs. They gave me looks of fear, anger, disgust, and curiosity. I tried to maintain an innocent look but couldn't help but feel like a wanted man in those handcuffs. Tanya had a chance to come to the holding cell before we left and I told her to fly back to Atlanta and find out what was going on. I would deal with Miami. Tanya was forced to fly home from her honeymoon by herself. She ended up throwing away a suitcase full of shoes because she couldn't carry it all.

Miami Dade County Jail looked like any other jail. I was searched and stripped. I had to put on this orange county inmate suite and await processing. I was so humiliated. The deputies at the jail didn't respect me at all. They assumed that I was just some convicted inmate trying to claim innocence. The attitudes of the correction officers were mostly negative.

"You shouldn't have done the crime! You wouldn't be here."

They didn't understand that this had to be a mistake nor did they care. They also entertained themselves by overextending their authority especially in front of the female correction officers. They seemed to be showing out for them or something. When my name was called for medical screening, one officer attempted to assert his authority by forcing me to walk around the holding room to get to the doctor instead of allowing me to just get out my chair and step four feet into the doctor's office. I ignored his demand and was quickly reprimanded, but the doctor overruled by saying, "We don't have all day for this nonsense. Let him into my office!"

I completed my medical screening and was placed in a holding cell for another eight hours until we were finally allowed to relocate upstairs with the other population. This was very hard on me emotionally. I was worried about Tanya and her emotions. I was trying to figure out why would Fulton County Superior Court want me back in jail? I completed the program as they requested. I was the star pupil in the program. They even asked me to speak. Why would they have a warrant for my arrest? I knew it would be hours before we would know anything. It was Saturday and the courts wouldn't be back in session until Monday. Once upstairs, it would be a few more hours before my number would be in the system to use the phone. Once I got my chance, I called Tanya. She had made it home safely. We talked for my allotted fifteen minutes. She said that she would go downtown first thing Monday morning and find out what was happening. I spent the whole day Sunday resting and worrying.

Monday morning arrived and the truth was sinking in more and more. I was in jail. This is a place I thought I would never see again. Count times, med calls, and chow time I just knew was a thing of the past for me. I became angry. Why was this happening? I asked myself at least a thousand times already. I knew I wouldn't reach my wife until the evening so I waited. Around noon, my name was called to go to court. This was a video court where you stood in front of a computer screen talking to the judge on the other end. As soon as my time came, I went to explain that this must be a mistake, but the judge interrupted and said that they could hold me up to fourteen days. If Fulton County didn't come to pick me up by then, they would release me. I panicked. Would I be in jail for the next fourteen days? Please, Lord, tell me this isn't so! I was returned to my cell where I waited until evening to speak with Tanya.

Finally, I got in touch with her around 5:30 that evening. She told me how this all came about. Apparently back in 2014, a district attorney from Fulton County felt that I had not properly dealt with drug possession case from 2011. It was a case that the judge dismissed for improper procedure on the officer's behalf. This districted attorney took it upon herself to re-indict me for this charge. They sent out the indictment to a homeless shelter that I lived in back in 2010. When there was no-show from me on the court date, they sat without my knowledge, they took a warrant out for my arrest. The problem with this is that there should have never been a warrant on a return mail court notice. It means that the person you're asking to come to court doesn't know they are supposed to be in court. They shared this information with Tanya. Tanya then went into the courtroom of the judge that signed the warrant, to share this discovery. I tell you, my wife played lawyer on this day. She was up by seven that morning and stayed in the courtroom all day until finally the court issued an immediate release form and faxed it to the Miami Dade County Jail.

God was at work this day because the officers of the court were very helpful and apologetic for this interrupted honeymoon, but I was still baffled at why would the district attorney seek me for a new case. All the people running around in the street breaking laws, and I was the primary focus of this district attorney! I became even more angry at this, relieved but angry. A few more hours passed and I decided I would call it a night. Maybe they would call my name in the morning. Fifteen minutes later, I got that announcement every confined inmate looks forward to "Graham, Benjamin, pack it up!"

I grabbed my belongings and headed for the security door. The whole releasing process would be another two hours. I was released around 9:00 p.m. Monday. They gave me a one-way bus pass. I asked about directions to the Miami airport. It didn't seem to be too far from the jail. I stared at this place from the window of my cell. I would walk if I had to. I called Tanya and we tried to figure out how to get me home without no credit cards or cash. The customs agent would not let me keep my cash or credit cards at the time of arrest. How hateful. It always amazes me at how people will do things to make your journey even more difficult, but every single time, God has shown up and showed out. While waiting on the bus to take me to the airport, a shuttle van pulled up. I never caught a bus in Miami before, so I assumed it was the bus. The driver told me that the bus to the airport stop running a few hours earlier, but he would give me a lift. I was a bit concern because there was no signs on this van to indicate he was a professional transportation person. When I got aboard, the driver told me what he does. He rides up and down this street during the night, picking up people who may need to be blessed with a ride. I became emotional. I knew God had sent this angel to give me a ride to the airport. God knew the busses wasn't coming and how frustrated I had become. The elderly gentleman explained that this was his ministry giving others a ride that needed it. He dropped me of within a mile of the airport and I walked the rest of the way there. I arrived around 11:00 p.m. Tanya had booked a flight online, but it wasn't due to leave until 7:00 a.m. I was stranded at the airport until that time. Excitement wouldn't allow me to sleep. I paced the airport until the AC inside the airport became unbearable. I still had on the shorts I was arrested in. I discovered it was warmer outside so I went out there and sat on a bench for the remaining hours. The ticket booths opened at 5:00 a.m. I confirmed my flight and headed to the gate.

Once at the gate, I still had several hours before the plane began the boarding process. I decided to take a snooze for a bit. Soon, I was in the air and on my way back to Atlanta. Once I arrived at Hartsfield Airport in Atlanta, I phoned Tanya to see where she would meet me. It was so awkward meeting my wife at the end of the honeymoon this way. We had plans on how we were going to spend a few hours in Miami before our flight left. Who could possibly imagine a honeymoon where the wife and husband are forced to separate from each other at the end? I hated the district attorney for this. You don't get moments like these back. This was also my first cruise so you can imagine the thoughts about the cruise ship. I worked hard at remaining humble during this trying time. We were not completely out the water yet either. The district attorney set a court day for me two weeks after I was released from the Miami Dade Jail.

The following week was back to business as Tanya and I opened the store. People were excited for us, but we couldn't help but feel cheated in some way. We did our best to go along with the excitement, but the truth is we both wanted to cry from the events that took place at the end of the honeymoon. Finally, I began to talk to others about what happen. I felt the need to share. It was starting to ball up in me and created this uncomfortable bitterness, that mad at the system type attitude. Rev Maker came into the store that week and he was one of the first ones I shared with. He knew a lot of people down at the Superior Court and I thought that he might be able to get to the bottom of this whole thing. Rev Maker was very upset when I told him what happen. He immediately made plans to go speak with the head of the district attorney's office. Before he went to meet with them, I gave him my file. It contain all the things that I had done since my initial release from Fulton County in 2011. I had completed their yearlong program with flying colors. I was chosen to speak at the graduation. I was even invited a year later to come out and speak to the other graduates of the program. I was even given a certificate by the court for remaining crime and drug free and being a role model in the community. I also included a list of places I had spoken such as Pacola Public Schools which included 800 students. Rev Maker took the file and headed downtown. The first day, he sat down with the head of the department. He was then scheduled an appointment to meet with the actual prosecutor handling my case.

By this time, others had heard about my issue and began to call the district attorney's office as well.

Everyone was shocked that charges were being brought against me for a case that was originally dismissed. Tanya and I continued to pray and go about our regular routine. The next day, Rev Maker went to meet with the prosecutor. She explained to Rev Maker that she felt that I had not dealt with this case and that I should. Rev Maker began to show her my file. He showed her the before and after picture. He told her that "This is not the same person as the one you seek on the before photo. This man is a pillar of the community. He is a role model and mentors many people in recovery. He went to school for counseling and also owns a convenience store on the same street he slept as a homeless man. And the worst part about this case is that the warrant you filed for his arrest ended up being served while he was on his honeymoon."

At the sound of all this, the district attorney put her head down. She didn't realize the wonderful things that had taken place in my life and what I was doing today. All she saw was another piece of paper that needed to be added to the conviction status from their office. Had she took time out to investigate the case she would have seen the things that Rev Maker shared with her. She apologize to Rev Maker for her part in my arrest and decided to file for an immediate dismissal. She gave Rev Maker a form and told him to take it to courtroom B. He took the paper as instructed and they began the process to dismiss this case. A few hours later, Rev Maker was in the store with Tanya and me sharing this experience. As Tanya and Rev Maker talked, I went in to bathroom and started crying.

"Lord, you did it again! Thank you!"

The next year would go by uneventful as far as disasters were concern. We did continue to grow in business and become a community resource for those in needs. We noticed during the summer that many of the homeless individuals were coming into the store thirsty. Tanya and I decided to start a free bottle water program. We simply bought a few cases of water and designated a shelf in one of the coolers to give out water. We ran an ad on social media and people began to bring cases of water by the store. We did the same things for socks and clothes. Things seem to fall in place. Not only were we meeting the needs of the community, but we also had a chance to minister to people on a regular basis. Eventually, several people were motivated forward. They got off the street and into a program and began their journey as I once did. Several organizations that provided assistance for me along the way invited me to come and share my story with their donors. I was glad to. I'm grateful at the help provided for me when I was ready for help. The City of Atlanta and its community partners certainly paved a way for me. Thank you, Lord.

CHAPTER 21

Finale

*"Humble yourselves under the mighty hand of the Lord
that He may exalt you in due time." (1 Peter 5:6)*

I t was the month of February 2017, and I received a call from the mayor's office. Tanya and I was invited to his annual State of the City address. They mention that the mayor would give recognition of my success. I was excited. "Lord, you have once again blessed my journey."

As I was thinking about this opportunity, an elderly lady walked into the store. She had been in the store several times over the past few years, but this time was different. She walked up to the counter and said, "Your momma's name is Margaret Graham."

I was shocked at this because I wondered how this lady would know my mother's name. I knew the lady to be a bit mental at times but how was she coming up with this information. Finally, it dawned on me that it was actually the Spirit of my mom sending a vibe to let me know that she was celebrating with me. I cried as the Spirit explain this to me.

The following morning of the address came, and Tanya and I headed out. The speech took place at a ballroom downtown. The mayor had actually reserved a table for his distinguished guests, and we were one of them! About three-fourths of the way through his speech, he spoke about my journey. He called my name and I stood up. As he told the audience how I went from sleeping under a bridge to now owning a store near that same bridge, they stood and applauded. I fought hard to hold back the tears. Our table was positioned next to a judiciary table which sat the head prosecutors and judges. During the course of the breakfast, I would stare over at that table. I wanted to tell them "thank you" for sentencing me to a program which saved my life, but was afraid to.

Benjamin and Tanya with Andrew Young former Mayor of Atlanta.

Benjamin and Tanya with Mayor Kasim Reed.

After the mayor's speech, the judges approached me. One of the judges was near tears. He jumped for joy as he shouted, "I know you! You were in my courtroom before."

I marveled at this. Who would have thought that this would come full circle and end on a note like this? This made that judge's day to see someone who was once in his courtroom for drug possession to now being honored by the mayor of Atlanta. We embraced and I made myself available to speak on future occasions.

That morning of recognition was one of God's way of saying, "Well done, my good and faithful servant."

There is a reason I named this book, *The Book of Benjamin*. Similar to the books in the Bible, we read about many people's journey as they walked according to their calling. I hope my story has inspired you to keep the faith during difficult times and also to be encouraged to pursue your dreams. It is possible. I love you. God bless.

About the Author

Benjamin Graham's story is being told all over the country by many. His journey of overcoming life's major obstacles has inspired many from those experiencing homelessness to even high-ranking officials. Benjamin sits on the board of Partners for Home Inc., a governing body for Atlanta's various Continuums of Care. He is also a successful business owner along with his lovely wife, Tanya Graham. Benjamin Graham is a cofounder of Motivation Forward Inc., a 501 (c) 3 non-profit organization responsible for outreach, mentoring, and assisting men and women of all ages that deal with addiction, mental illness, and homelessness. He often speaks at court programs, schools, colleges, churches, and other non-profit organizations concerning drug use and its dangers. He also uses motivational entertainment as a public speaking tool to engage and inspire. Benjamin Graham was recently recognized by Atlanta's Mayor Kasim Reed for his amazing accomplishments.

CPSIA information can be obtained
at www.ICGtesting.com
Printed in the USA
FSHW04n1329150318
45488FS